NO
Turning Back

Stephen S. Fisher

ISBN 978-1-0980-2266-2 (paperback)
ISBN 978-1-0980-2267-9 (digital)

Christian Faith Publishing, Inc.
832 Park Avenue
Meadville, PA 16335
www.christianfaithpublishing.com

Printed in the United States of America

My wife and I have had many journals from our fifty-three years in Africa. Then my wife took sick and was diagnosed with stage IV cancer, and we quickly and abruptly left the country of Africa in search of treatment for my precious wife. In the process, the journals were left behind, and I do not have access to them now. What a loss but for the glory of God. When my wife graduated and went to glory, I said, now I must write a book just to tell you of the present moves of God and the blessing that my wife and I shared together. Now I must put them on paper, or they will be lost forever. So it is my hope and trust in the Lord that as you read these testimonies—for they are true and we have seen them firsthand—that they will inspire you, challenge you, and be a blessing to you. Lord willing, I will be continuing at least two more books to contain more of God's blessings and to tell the world the greatness of our God that has no limitations. So may your inspiration and your commitment to serve the Lord in a greater measure run high. May the Lord bless you richly, and may the testimony of your life become as a fire that burns off the trash and remains with a shining light. God bless you!

In the beginning was the word, and the Word was with God, the word was God. He was in the beginning with God. Everything came into being through the word. And without the word, nothing came into being. What came into being through the word was life, and the life was the light for all people.

—John 1:1–4

I was born on July 18, 1941, in the middle of a hot summer and during World War II. And what I was going to experience now is the story I am about to tell you.

Mother told me I was the only one of the children that has a memory of things that happened before I was one year old. When this started, I don't know. But the thing that I remember is how mother cared for me in the winter. I was a very gregarious person, even in my early age. I would always uncover myself and get my hands outside of the cover, then I would get cold even as a young baby. So mother thought of how to keep my hands from uncovering myself. This was her plan: she got an empty flour bag and sewed a lip in the open end of the bag then put a string inside the lip. She would place me inside the bag and pull the string just snugly around my neck and tie it in a slipknot outside of the bag. I was unable to get my hands outside, and therefore, I would not uncover myself. Wow! What a clever idea, but I hated that string around my neck restricting my liberty, and so I would scream and kick as I did not like it at all. I guess at an early age, I thought I was someone special. So I had quite a performance.

But my performance was very short-lived. My father soon sorted out my problem by teaching me that he was the boss and not me. He applied the thirty-six inches of a yardstick that measured correction to my posterior piece of learning possibility. And the battle was over. That is the first lesson that I remember learning. Needless to say, many were the times when I was corrected, and many were the times when Dad would have to remind me that there were rules. Slowly, I began to learn. I remember playing with my siblings on the floor of our house. We did not have a lot of toys. During World War II, things were very complex and difficult.

We didn't have much variety. But we had lots of fun. We had some cuts of wood that we use for blocks to play with. We played many different games. We even had some dolls to play with. We had individual names for all them. These were homemade dolls, and they were filled with sawdust. It was terribly dirty when they began to leak but otherwise a lot of fun. We played with them, as though they were real people, and we had a hilarious time.

We would go to the barn and play with the baby sheep and the baby calves and the chickens. The only problem with the chickens was we would frighten them. They would fly, and if they would fly away, we were in big trouble. So Dad had to remind us of the rules and some things we do not do! And so we learn to not get into trouble. I don't know why I went to church when I was young. Every Sunday, I would get into trouble. And then it caused me pain. What a conniving schemer I was, just too intelligent for my size. I don't know where I learned to do what I did. But I'm sure until then I had never read the rule book. Anyway, finally, I think I've grown up, at least somewhat.

Unorthodox Ways at Sikalongo Mission

A t the mission, we have twenty-two pigs to help sustain the mission. It has a farm and two milk cows. With that, you are in charge of the mission, the school, and the hospital. Shirley Heisey was the nurse at the hospital. She was a few years my senior and complained at my administration. The bishop soon set that straight. He told her I am the superintendent and that was final. We had no more problems with that. I set out immediately with the African overseer's son to begin to evangelize the area. Two days a week, I spent in the field to evangelize the area. My fractured back took another two years to heal. Paul Muleya and I went out on my motorcycle and preached the gospel. Then I begin to zero in like a radar on those people called the backsliders. My question was, who are the backsliders? It was invariably a man that had taken more than one wife. Big whoop, this was their culture! Why have they backslidden? As I begin to question these individuals, I realized they have never slid forward! Now when have you ever accepted Jesus Christ as your Lord and Savior?

In 1929, I became a member of the church. It was the prerequisite to become eligible to become a teacher. To be a member, they use the term *repent*. I did not know what it meant, but that is what I had to do to become a member, so I did that. The following year, I was baptized, then I became a member. The following year, I worked at the mission. The next year, I did some teacher training and became a teacher. When I had come this far and I was teaching school, I began to make a bit of money, and that was nice. Then the people of my culture began to talk to me saying, "You must take another wife." This is who we are. You are living in Africa, so be an African. You are not a white man. So I took the second wife and soon the third wife. Then I was called a backslider. My membership of the church was revoked. I was in this mess, and there is no redemption. "So very typical!"

Paul was the son of an early convert of the early missionaries. His father taught his children biblically. Paul was a big help to me during my three years of ministry there. He was my interpreter, and the work flourished and went forward. I know we ministered to many, many, many, many, many, many backsliders. And most of them accepted the Lord for the first time in their life. They each became a child of God as we had the joy and opportunity of bringing many of them to faith in Jesus Christ. With this evangelistic approach, I was not a popular missionary. I was labeled an unorthodox missionary who needs to understand the Word of God properly. The work was growing, and many people were coming to faith in Jesus Christ. And it was very exciting.

The work flourished, and many people came to faith in Christ. When I first began to approach the backsliders, it was not easy. The missionaries had rejected them for their lifestyle and labeled them backsliders. Fair enough, but what about their soul. So I pursued with great success. First, the wives would accept Jesus, then after a period of time, some of the husbands also accepted Jesus as Lord and Savior of their life, and things begin to happen.

Believe me, I was not popular, they would rather discard me and also labeled me a backslider. God was not finished with me yet. And so we pursued, and the blessing of the Lord followed. And the work grew as there were new converts all over the place. Yes, it was hard work, but God was blessing our efforts. My dear wife at this time was working at the hospital and doing a lot of hours at work there. I was developing the mission as it had run in the red for many years. Now I was supposed to be the miracle worker, but my ministry was unorthodox. And I was not a popular person. God was not finish with me yet. So I continued and started new churches in seven different locations in the next three years. God was on the move. Signs, wonders, and miracles were seen all the time, and to me, it was very exciting. I was growing up with many new challenges. And so the work went forward. One day, we were preaching at the village where an old evangelist lived. His name was Sampson Nlovu.

As we were preaching in his village, a young man about thirty-two years of age came riding into his village on a bicycle. His father, a very old man, rode on the back of the bicycle. The mother was walking behind and came in about fifteen minutes later. In the village, they all sat in the shade. We gave to them a simple Bible message and gave an invitation for anyone that would like to accept Jesus Christ as their Lord and Savior and to make Jesus the Lord of their life. The young men and women quickly accepted the invitation. The father said, "I am blind, I am old, my skin is old, my bones are old, and if I accept your invitation, it would only add to my sorrow as I am too old."

I asked his wife, the mother of the young man. She said, "Yes, I would like to." We then prayed, and she prayed a very beautiful prayer of repentance. And the two expressed the great joy they had in their life now.

Again, I approached the father. He said, "Yes, if you mean like that, then I am ready to pray." He then prayed a beautiful prayer. He was old, and he was blind, but he beautifully accepted Jesus and made him the Lord of his life.

The next week when we visited them in the village, the old man said this, "Mwame" (my master). The first time I ever prayed in my life was when we were in Sampsons Village. But when we came home, my wife and I began to talk as this is the only wife I ever had. We were talking. We sat down to take food. I told my wife we needed to pray and thank Jesus for the food. Before we went to bed, I said we need to thank Jesus for the good day we had. Then we slept all night. When we got awake in the morning, we thanked the Lord for the night of sleep. Now we pray before we take food, and we pray before we go to bed, and we pray when we get up in the morning. And God is with us all the time. I said to Paul, "Who is this old man!"

We talked to the father of Paul. He was about seventy-four years old. He said, "When I was just a small boy, that man was already an old man. And he was known as Chief Cheannamier." We asked him if he knows his age as he was very old. He did not know the year he was born. But he said this, "When I was a young boy, maybe eighteen years old, I fought again the Ndabalies when they came to fight against the Lozie and the Tonga Tribe here in this country." You can look in the encyclopedia and see when the British troops intervened and stopped this tribal war. We did a bit of calculation and suggested that this man, at this time, may be 120 years old. By looking at the year 1970 and him having been a young man during that time, he was approximately 120 years. The next time we came to his village, he had a new revelation that he spoke to us about.

He said, "Missionary, is it a sin for me to use tobacco?" Now how do you answer a question like that? I needed to be biblically correct.

I answered, "The Word says if you misuse or abuse your body, God will destroy you."

He looked to his wife and answered, "We have been chewing tobacco. But it is not food—it is not something that we need. So we stop."

And I stopped. I did not use tobacco anymore. I didn't tell them it was bad or that I desired otherwise. The Holy Spirit told him. God is so amazing. I am so convinced that God is more concerned about men and unrighteousness and that he is more willing to forgive them for their sin than to judge them for their unrighteousness. God loves his creation. And he desires for them to flourish in righteousness, in the kingdom of God, right here on earth! Hallelujah!

There was this little old man who went to visit Chief Cheannamier. As he was walking nearby his village, he stopped in for a cup of water and talked with the old chief. The old chief had now found Jesus as his Lord and Savior. His life had changed. He said to the old man, "You also are an old man, and you do not know the day that you will die. *You too* need to accept Jesus Christ as your Lord and Savior. That is what I have done just a short time ago." The old man then asked how he could do that. The chief said he did not know, but if you go to Sikalongo Mission, there is a missionary there that will tell you how to become a child of God. I would be happy to tell you, but I do not know the way, the missionaries can tell you. The day that old man came to the mission, I was in town, I think Paul was at the mission at the time as he was in charge of the mission store. The old man talked with someone at the mission. He said he had come to find out how to become a Christian. Chief Cheannamier said that he needs to become a child of God and the missionary can tell him how to become one. He did not explain where he lives, except that he is in the Sciaswela Area and that his name is Cabbage. When I came back from town, they told me the story of this old man who came to the mission and asked for the missionary. I asked where he lived. They said somewhere in Sciaswela.

Sciaswela is only an area. So how can I find this man? This place is in the bush, and the bush is huge and dark. How would I find him? But we were desperate. So we got on my motorcycle, and Paul and I began to look for this man. We started by asking people along the path leading to Sciaswela if yesterday they found an old man walking along the path. No one had seen him. We continued to go and ask more people if they have seen an old man walking along this path. We continued for a few hours, desperately trying to find this old man that had come to mission to find out how to become a Christian. By late in the afternoon, we were nearly exhausted. We asked at many villages if anyone had seen this old man by the name of Cabbage. Finally, one man said, "Yes, there is an old man by the name of Cabbage. He lives on the left side of the mountain road in a small village, and he has many goats. His name is Cabbage, and he is quite an old man."

Well done and we said, "Thank you very much." We went in search of his village and found the man named Cabbage. When we found him late in the afternoon, it was time to return to the mission. We were nearly one hour away. We began to talk to him. He told us he had been to the Village of Cheannamier.

Two days before he had gone to see the chief, he went to the mission but did not find the missionary there, so he returned to his village, and that is where we found him. He had many goats, there was goat manure everywhere. You couldn't walk anywhere without tramping in goat manure. It was one dirty village. But in this very primitive village, there lived an old man. He was dirty. He too had not washed for a long time. And his hut was dirty. But in his heart, he was hungry for truth. And he went to find the missionary that could help him to have faith in Jesus Christ. And now the missionary has arrived. We talked at length about his life and about where he hoped to go from here even though it was late. We took time to talk to him. It was decision-making time. I was really excited to give him until he wants no more. We talked to him about his life. He was hungry, he was dirty, and he did not smell nice, but he needed Jesus, and his heart was hungry. We asked him if he knew where he would go when he died. He said, "Into the ground."

"But where is your spirit going?"

"Into the ground."

We explained to him God's plan of salvation. He did not have a Bible, and he did not know the way. We explained carefully to him God's plan of salvation. Jesus died on the cross not because he was tired of living but because men could not save themselves. The wages of sin is death. So Jesus died, so we don't have to die. But the gift of God is eternal life. And he graciously and willingly accepted Jesus Christ as his Lord and Savior. It was not the scripture and verse that was necessary for this man to understand. For he did not know the scripture. "But the word of God, the mighty word of God is alive an active! It is sharper than any two edged sword. It penetrates even to separating the soul from the spirit. It will separate the joints from the marrow of the bone. It judges the thoughts and attitudes of the heart. Nothing in all creation is hidden from God's sight. Everything is uncovered and laid bare before the eyes of God. To Him, we must give account" (Heb. 4:12–13). Hallelujah!

The three years that we worked at Sikalongo Mission, I was developing a pig farm. I was seeing the potential to make money and get the mission out of debt. It had been in the hole too long. With my understanding of raising pigs, I decided that I could soon get the mission out of the red. At this time, we were making bricks to build a new primary school on the upper side of the dam. I carried a wagon load of broken bricks that they could not be used for building, and I brought them to the mission. Then I begin to build a pig parlor, like my father had once built. After we finished constructing this pig pen, I cemented the floor, and soon, the building was ready for pigs. I did not have enough pigs to fill the parlor as it could house forty pigs. So I bought a lot of young pigs from the local villagers. I wormed the pigs and then put them in the parlor until they were growing up to 170 pounds. Then I would take them to market. This plan worked well. In the meantime, I kept all the good females for reproducing. At the end of three years, I had more than three hundred pigs. I would sell about ninety pigs every month to the capital city. I would sell six to the local butcher in town every week. A few months after I started fattening pigs on the large scale, I saw how well this was going to work. The church executive board allowed me to buy my own two-ton truck. I put a second floor on the back of the truck so I could take a larger amount of pigs to town. I would take a big truck load of about ninety to the capital city every month.

We were beginning to make money. Soon, the debt was paid off. For the first time in a long time, the mission was debt free. During this time, I was buying pigs from the local villagers. I would worm them (as they were full of worms) and then put them in with the other pigs to grow them up. It was a new ministry to the villagers. And it brought many people to faith in Christ. A butcher in the capital city was so excited about my pigs. Even if there were twenty trucks lined up waiting to off-load their pigs, they would see my truck. They would then come to me and say, "Your truck is next," and I would pass all the other trucks up, and I would off-load next. Such favor the Lord showed us. The work was hard and long. But the blessing of God was with us. And people were continually getting saved and delivered.

When I would start another church, I would look for a pastor. At this time, Jacob Muchimba was the man feeding the pigs. He was doing a very good job. He had Bible school training but never was utilized. I put him in charge of one of my churches. That was not Orthodox, as Jacob had never been assigned to a place to preach.

But he was very happy, and his church was growing. I was always reaching out.

We went to Sinazongwe, a huge village right on the Zambezi River. It was near the edge of Lake Kariba, a man-made lake by the British government. At this village, it was hot, and the people lived in small huts about twelve feet off the ground. The people only wore a G-string as it was too hot to wear clothing. When I was preaching there, many of these people came to faith in Jesus Christ. They were very excited.

On the outside of the village, among the rocks, there was a troop of baboons. They would sit there mocking us. The Word of God was preached, the baboons mocked us, and the people heard the Word of God. They came to faith in Jesus Christ. But not one of the baboons understood the gospel. We have been "asleep" too long! We must wake up! We did not come from monkeys as scientists would have us believe. We are the creation of God himself. This was very much verified there, for the baboons never came to faith in Christ. Man does not come from the monkeys. Both are the creation of God. But monkeys do not have a soul, and therefore, we are separate from the animals. These people were special, and a church was born there. People, without wearing clothing, came to faith in Christ. They became a gracious people. I remember one chief there, he had thirty wives and about three hundred children. Oh, the era of man. God, have mercy upon the human race. But many of these people came to faith in Jesus Christ. What a marvel. God is just so amazing! Praise the name of Jesus! I think there were about 130 people at the church.

And then there was Amos Munsaka, he was a dear old brother who also came down through the ranks of time, as so many others that became a member of the church but never really had faith in Jesus Christ. Yes, they changed the way they live. They became a church member through baptism so they could become a schoolteacher. It was a way for man to gain clout and improve their way of life. I believe for them to become a church member, this was a process to help them to improve their way of life. It was of value, as they could go to school and get an education and have many benefits. A person who has nothing can improve his stature and become someone. This is what they all wanted. He became a schoolteacher after he had come through to the rank and file. First, he needed to repent, then the next year, he became eligible for baptism, then he became a member of the church, then he went for teacher training and became a schoolteacher.

It was a long process, but it was worth it as now they could draw a salary. It was an improvement in their life style. But with all this, he did not make Jesus the Lord of his life. He was still a weak individual when culture issues would arise.

Let me say something here: culture and tradition are a big issue! Many times, it is more powerful than the church. They have to make decisions. Jesus is not the Lord of their life, so what shall they choose—culture and tradition or the church? This is where these men were held in a trap. They choose culture. They take another wife. And rightfully so, they are expelled from the church.   B u t they are still lost and taking away their church membership, and they leave the church. This is one issue. Who will redeem them? They have been told they have to repent. They say I have done that before. I became a *church member* (whatever that word means), but they are still lost! And so life goes on, and they live a life of tradition and culture. And sin begets sin. And when sin gives birth, it gives birth to death! That is what my Bible says. So their life goes on. They are now separated from the church, they have no church fellowship, they have no Christian relationship. Bring the little bit of fervor they had in their life. There eventually and completely burned out. And they have no desire for righteous living.

I said Amos, but Jesus died for you, and he shed his blood on Calvary, this he did for a specific reason. The Bible says the wages of sin is death. Jesus died for you, so you do not have to die.

If you accept the sacrifice that Jesus made at Calvary, if you believe that Jesus Christ is the Son of God, then you shall be saved! He heard the words that I spoke. And he said, "But, Umfandise (pastor), you do not understand, for I am a backslider, and for me there is no forgiveness, I repented once, now look where I am."

I asked again, "Do you believe that Jesus Christ is the Son of God!"

"Yes, Umfandise, I do."

"Do you believe that God raised him from the dead and that he ascended to heaven?"

"Yes, Umfandise, I do believe that!"

"Have you asked Jesus to forgive you of your sin? Can I ask him to forgive me for my sins?"

"Yes, please do!"

Then we prayed. His face lit up. And it would seem that for the first time. His sin was under the blood of Jesus. And it would seem as though now he was born again, and his life radically changed. That was on a Tuesday. Late the following Friday, he died and went to be with Jesus. Another soldier down, he suffered long, and he fought hard. There are many such men. I began to reach out to them and to evangelize their life. Usually, the man was the last to except Jesus. Often, one of the wives would first accept Jesus and then the second and the third and fourth wife; in many cases, the fifth also. When they came to faith in Jesus Christ, then they were changed, and so it was many, many times, as many were the backsliders, just to say they live a rejected, neglected life. When I began to court these people, I was termed an unorthodox missionary. But to me, it was the Word of God. So orthodox or unorthodox, I became a fervent proclaimer of the Word of God. And God always gets the glory and adds the increase.

Let me tell you about Pastor Mushanga. One day, five vehicles drove into our mission at Chibangu. I went to see what is the performance. They said we are all pastors from one church, the BIC Church. We have started two churches in the local vicinity, and we are having a conference. "Since we have traveled a long ways, can we kindly ask for a drink of water?"

"Yes, my friends, come on in."

We gave them water freely. As they sat in the living room. They began to introduce themselves. All them were originally from the southern province of Zambia, and they had names familiar to my ear.

As from 1963 to 1965, I was building Choma Secondary School; then in 1969, again, we went to southern province and spent three years in service there. It was during this period of time that I was reaching these polygamous for Jesus Christ! So the names were familiar with me. Then one pastor said, "My name is Pastor Mushanga. I am pastor of the BIC Church in Kitwe. I said you address me as Mr. Fisher, but how do you know who I am."

"Your name, Mushanga, the only Mushanga that I know, was a man that lives near Mboli, and his name was William Mushanga."

"Yes, he said, William is my father, and I am the last-born son of the fifth wife of William."

Wow! And how well I remember the day I went to speak to William and ask him why he is in such a state. I am a backslider. There is no hope for me. We talked at length. He was a schoolteacher. He was an educated man but never made Jesus Christ the Lord of his life. I took him through the Scriptures; the Word of God is sharper than any two-edged sword—the Word of God, yes, the Word of God. I know we use it so little. I explained to him the plan of salvation. He said that is not for me. I am a sinner, there is no forgiveness for me. I am a backslider. I wanted to cry. He would not make any decision for Jesus that day. He said I am a backslider and, therefore, there is no hope for me. I talked with him at length and then asked if I can talk to his wife. She was gracious and hungry for the Word of God. She said, "Mumfandise, what can I do to be saved?" I took time to explain to them the Word of God. After a long conversation with the five wives, with hunger and with grace, they one by one asked Jesus to forgive them of their sin. And they accepted Jesus Christ as their Lord and Savior! They were changed forever. Many times, I went to visit them. They were hungry for the Word of God. And they desired rich fellowship. We had many good times together. And now here is this man this unorthodox missionary, bringing new life to lost souls. And what a joy it was to me! Here is the last-born son of the fifth wife, of this man William Mushanga, the backslider, who thought that there was no hope for him who also came to faith in Jesus Christ. After all, his wives had excepted Jesus, and his heart was finally made soft by the joy and relationship that his wives had with Jesus. Hallelujah! It was time to celebrate! Thank you, Jesus, for the cross! Thank you for saving the impossible. And thank you, Jesus, for giving me love for my fellowman. Thank you for giving me a love for those who persecute me and think that I am unorthodox. You see, my friend, my life is not my own. I've been bought by the blood of Jesus. He canceled my sin and took away all my guilt. And for that, I owe him my life. So my life I have given to him for the past fifty-three years, living in Africa to proclaim the Gospel, the good news. Jesus came to give us life. I know that we can have it more in abundance, hallelujah! Jesus is the Waymaker, he makes a way where there is no way. He is the Lord, he is commander-in-chief, and he is sovereign. He changes not, and his ways are past finding out! Halleluiah! Jesus is Lord! He is the Alpha and Omega! And he reigns forever and ever and ever. Amen! Hallelujah! (Romans 11:3)

And now here are these people, about forty-five years later, they stopped in our place and asked for a glass of water. Is it really worth the hard life, having survived two road accidents, having lived through four wars, and having survived a ten-day hostage situation, and now having given up my wife? Is that really worth it all? The world is still lost and going to hell. What can I do today to make the Word of God more affective? Even if I give my life to be burned and I persecuted myself, if I do not have love, then I am an empty drum. And I only resonate a loud doom. Let us do the will of the Father and tell the world that Jesus Christ is Lord! In Word and in deed! Amen.

Allow me to tell you a little bit about Arron Ressler. He is one very special individual, who grew up as a horse and buggy Mennonite, a walk of life, simulator to the Amish, with a few technical doctrinal differences, but with a strong faith in God. He had become a member of the worship center and interdenominational charismatic church that grew out of the 1970s charismatic renewal. It was the church we were members of for some years before we went to Zaire. Arron came to work with us as a young committed volunteer, and what a blessing he was. There was nothing mechanical that he could not do. He could fix motor vehicles, fix motors, do welding jobs. He was excellent, and him and our son were a team to behold. At the same time, Corina Snyder also volunteered to come and work with us and work with Mom. What a committed servant she was too, as nothing she was asked to do, she was not willing to do. We were living in the Bush where life is quite primitive. But we always have a good time. In the evening, we would play games and watch videos. We made up a lot of our own functions. Really we had a good time. And Carina was a special member of our family too. I do not have enough old newsletters to remember all the stories that I need to tell, but what I remember about Arron, I guess, is all the good things that we did together. One time I went to town with the Unimog. When I came to the first river at Chasambale, we had not gone into town for about two months. And this bridge was about fifty feet long. And some kind person had come along and stolen all the planks and metal sheets that were making it possible for someone to cross the bridge. All these things were gone, and it was not possible to cross. So I turned around and went home and asked Mahlon and Arron to get the chain saws and fuel and oil for the sawmill and go with me to the mountain, as we want two cut new planks for the bridge, as someone has stolen everything that was on top of the bridge. So we headed for the mountain with provisions for the day. Mom and Carina were busy in the hospital.

So we went to one mountain, and we began to cut some very big trees as big as we could cut in the saw. So I cut a load of planks three inches thick and eighteen inches wide and eighteen feet long. What massive planks these were. We would cut a tree down and drive right along side off the tree with the sawmill, and the tree was lying on the ground. We put a chain underneath the log, hooked one end of the chain on the sawmill frame and the other end on the Unimog, having a chain run from the sawmill, underneath the log, and up over the sawmill and onto the vehicle. Then we put the ramps next to log onto the sawmill. Then I would pull on the chain with the vehicle, and the tree would roll up the ramp on to the bed of the sawmill. It worked excellent. Then I would cut the pieces of wood to put it on the bridge. The bridge had an I-beam ten inches thick every ten feet across the whole length of the bridge. So the planks were massive as they were eighteen-feet-long, three-inch-thick-by-eighteen-inch-wide planks. We would then slide them onto the back of the vehicle, and when we had a load, we would then go down to the bridge and slide them off the back of the Unimog and on to the ten-inch I-beams, which were at eight-foot intervals.

The planks were long enough to cover three times I-beams, but I cut them three inches thick as they were so heavy, I said no one will ever steal them. I cut enough for the whole length of the fifty-foot-long bridge and put two wide for each wheel. That was three feet wide for each wheel. So now it was easy to cross the bridge. Then at the end of each length of each piece of plank, three inches from the end, I drilled 3 one-half-inch holes and then threaded thread pieces of number 9 wire and threaded it to both ends of the plank now resting on the I beam, so the planks cannot separate from driving over them and causing an accident. It took us, I think, three days to complete this task, but it looked like a job well done. I said at least we will never have to fix this bridge again as my reasoning was, they were too heavy for anyone to carry off and heavy, we worked like troopers. And we had made a good bridge. But much to my surprise, thieves will always surprise you, my Bible says it like this. All things are possible to them the belief. Believe what? I say this, and I hear what the Bible says, and I believe it very much. But in Africa, believe in it or do not believe in it, it is still possible! As I was coming back from town, one week later, they had already started stealing the planks. They would take an ax and cut the planks into pieces to use it for a table. What a surprise!

October 18

So that was another great job complete. I crossed the bridge and went to town. I went to town, ended my one-week business, and returned home with a truckload of supplies. But again, I was unable to cross the bridge. So I drove down the river a little bit further, and there drove through the river, up the other side, and went on home. You have to do what you have to do. And for the next few times, we drove through the river. We had taken the sawmill back to the mission. And men were working on building the new mission. Times were quite crucial. Work often was hard. But we never stopped reaching out. Mom was busy at the hospital. And the blessing of God was with the work, and so we had to on a daily basis. Take the Word of God and make it work in our life. And that is how we continued: build bridges and major roads, travel to the unknown, and take the good news of the Gospel of Jesus Christ to the whole world.

Travel in Times of War

In 1978, we were traveling on our way to put our son in school in South Africa. You see, as missionaries, things are not always ideal, so we have to do what we have to do to give our children the best education we can. And that is not always easy.

At this point in time, we were traveling all over Zambia, preaching and teaching wherever we went.

In 1975, I had purchased a Mercedes-Benz delivery van with a 220 diesel in it. I bought it in the town of Kitwe. Then I built onto the inside, which was thirteen feet of van space, a complete motor home. The dining room table would fold down to a bed where Mom and I would sleep comfortably in a double-size bed. There were two complete bunks. Pauline was with us at this time, she and Mahlon slept on the two bunks. Rob was also with us at this time, and he slept on the front seat. We had a two-burner gas stove and a small gas fridge. We had five gallons of drinking water storage that worked on an air pressure system, a basin for the sink that had a drain that would go outside. Needless to say, it was very handy indeed.

Then we traveled to South Africa to put our son in school. We had hidden in the back a cylinder of acetylene and a cylinder of oxygen. That's great for making repairs whenever it was necessary. This was a great blessing to us all the time. This allowed for free travel across borders without any problem as it was not exposed. It was inside a special little hidden cabinet in the back, just inside the back door.

The border between Zambia and Rhodesia was closed. So we had to go via Botswana and then back into Rhodesia. Then we traveled from Victoria Falls, south on the road to Bulawayo. This stretch of road was far, and it had only one gas station along the way. It was at a place called halfway house. We arrived there about 4:30 in the afternoon.

The commanding officer came to me. He said, "Where on God's earth have you come from?"

I said we have come from Victoria Falls. He said that it is not possible today. Just this afternoon, we have had seven terrorist attacks on that road. You say you have just traveled on the road now and you have not had any trouble? Someone bigger than you was looking after you.

I said we serve a God bigger than the god of this world! He said for sure that is true. We had seven ambushes on that road today. Again, we see that God is amazing. We had supper at the restaurant, we slept in the Motor Home, then had breakfast in the morning, then we left in a convoy with the military's convoy.

As we traveled to Bulawayo, the military convoy broke off after about thirty miles. They felt it was safe from there on, so we journeyed onward on our own.

After we had traveled about fifty miles, we developed engine problems. Remember, this was during the time of war. Now we were on our own with a broken-down vehicle in the middle of the war-torn country. The terrorists in the area were not nice to white people. All we could do was pray. We sat there in the middle of a war-torn country, not knowing what our next step was when suddenly an army truck came by. It was an army truck from the Rhodesian security forces. The truck stopped, it had seven officers on the truck. Immediately, six of them deployed themselves in the bush. The commander came to me and said, "What is your problem?"

He was a mechanic and a son of a spirit-filled father living in Bulawayo. I had a box of tools, and he went right to work, opened the valve cover of the motor, and found that I had dropped a valve on the number 3 piston.

He then said, "You will have to have your vehicle towed into the city of Bulawayo." That is more than one hundred miles away, so we waited. A truck came by, but he would not stop. After about fifteen minutes, another truck came by. This time, the officer used his rifle and stopped the truck and said he must tow me into the city.

This time, the officer used his authority, and the truck stopped. He towed us into the city without any question. We then telephoned the officer's father who also was a mechanic.

This family also was a spirit-filled Christian family. It was so delightful to meet other Christians, someone of like faith in the middle of a war-torn country. War is not nice, but to see how amazing God is, is just to phenomenal.

I think we stayed with this family for about four days as we had the motor repaired. Most of the work was done by this dear brother's father that we met on the road. He was one of the security forces. Now his parents became very dear friends of ours.

God is so amazing; the family of God is big even in a time of war. Many people died during this war, but God graciously spared our lives, as he was not finish with us yet. God is amazing!

After we had the motor repaired, we then journeyed south toward Beitbridge, the border crossing into South Africa, as this border was open. From there, we journeyed to Pietersburg, the first large city inside South Africa.

It was just before Christmas, so Anita spent her first Christmas with Harry van Hyestein and their family. Harry was the chapter president of the Full Gospel Businessmen in that city.

After we spent some time with them, we then journeyed going to Johannesburg.

After spending a few days with the Full Gospel Businessmen in Johannesburg and Willie Roeland, we went on to Pietermaritzburg where we were putting our son into boarding school.

In Pietermaritzburg, we found a family at a full gospel church there that adopted Mahlon as their child. While he was in boarding school and on weekends, he would stay with them and then go to church with them. This was a big consolation to us and a big help in our situation. We did not know anyone before that time in this city.

The father of this family was a high-ranking police officer in that city. He too was a mechanic, and he helped us with some engine problems that we were having. He said that I need to exchange the

timing chain in my engine with a timing gear. There we found a tractor motor that was the same as the motor I had. I bought the timing
gear, and we installed it. We had no more problems with that motor,
as previously the timing chain jumped a few links. And that was what
was causing my problem.

Now with that problem behind us, we again went back to
Johannesburg and spent a few days there and then once again to
Petersburg. After spending a few days, there we journeyed back to
the Rhodesia border.

After spending some days with our friends in Bulawayo and had
the motor fixed, I had gone to Salisbury to get a visa to go to South
Africa. I stayed there with the pastor's wife, of a church, a friend in
Zambia told us about. The pastor and the assistant pastor were not
there at the time as they had gone to a neighboring city with the
assistant pastor for a youth conference.

As we were sharing with the pastor's wife and the wife of the
assistant pastor about the experiences that we were having in Zambia,
at that time in Zambia, we were seeing many miracles. It was war-
time, and God was moving by his spirit.

At the supper table that evening, the pastor's wife said, "We
have a young man in our church who was fighting in the security
forces, and he was in a terrorist attack."

The security forces had stopped to make some tea, and now they
were putting their things away and were ready to go into action again.
There was an ambush waiting for them. As soon as they had put their
things away and they were now ready to move, seven terrorists in
the ambush, which were not seen before, now began throwing hand
grenades. The security forces hit the deck, and Raul landed on a hand
grenade, and it detonated at his throat. His whole bottom jaw is missing, and his voice box is very injured. Tomorrow morning at seven,
they are going to do the surgery and remove the rest of his voice box
and reconstruct another jawbone. He will never speak again.

"Stephen, since you are familiar with miracles, which we also
believe in, for the family it is a very sorrowful time, will you go along
to the hospital and pray for his healing?"

I agreed, but I did not know the family.

When we arrived at the hospital, eleven members of the family were standing around the hospital room. It was a hard time for all them. Not knowing them, I prayed in a very simple prayer. I don't remember the words that I used. But anyway, I prayed and we left the room that evening, only believing God for a miracle.

I did not know the family, but the pastor's wife told me he was a faithful member of the church, that he loves Jesus. We prayed for him again at the house before we went to bed. We went to bed and slept the night.

The next morning at the breakfast table, we were sitting there eating breakfast, and the telephone rang about seven o'clock. Pastor's wife answered the phone. She began crying as she was speaking on the phone. We did not know who called, so we did not know how to react to the situation.

She then hung up the phone. Regaining her composure, she then said, "Raul went in for surgery to have his voice box removed, as it was very damaged from the blast of the grenade."

But as the surgeon opened his throat again, the doctor exclaimed, "There is a complete and made whole voice box in his throat. I do not understand what has taken place. God has done a miracle. We do not have to remove his voice box as it is whole and complete."

Needless to say, we were invited back to visit on our return from South Africa.

With our son in school and no desperate emergency in front of us, we stayed for one week at this church and ministered there, going out and ministering to groups of people who were meeting on the rocks around the city and experiencing a tremendous move of God!

After staying there one week, we then wanted to go back to Zambia. So we made preparations to leave, and then a strange thing occurred. The security forces had crossed into Botswana in hot pursuit after a bunch of terrorists who were planting landmines in the area. Now all the borders were closed into neighboring countries. It was impossible for us to go anywhere. So the pastor said, "Stay a few weeks and see what the situation is then." We stayed and continue to minister in the city of Salisbury. Every day, we saw a great manifestation of the Spirit of God.

Then the pastor said, "The borders are not opening, so I think you need to stay here." And that is what we felt the Lord was saying for that time. We should stay there and work in Rhodesia.

There was nothing immediate that we had to go back to Zambia for, so we just stayed there for the time being to see where God is going to lead us next.

We then stayed in Rhodesia and ministered there for the next nine months. Eventually, things became very desperate, and it became very stressful for us even though things had gone well. Ministry was good. Miracles were plenty, and God was on the move!

We had to go to the ministry of immigration every day and see if they were still allowing us to stay in the country since we had chosen to stay in the country and do ministry there in Rhodesia.

We went to South Africa and collected our son from school. There was a good school for him to go to in Salisbury. But when we traveled to South Africa, there was a misunderstanding at the border, and they took away from us our permanent residency permit that we had previously. On our return, we no longer had our permanent residency. Now we had to go every week and check to see if our visa had been renewed. Finally, we decided to just go home to America.

We entered the challenge again of making preparations to leave the country, this time by flight. This too was a hassle. To have money transferred into Rhodesian money was not acceptable. The world had sanctioned Rhodesia, and America would not send money into Rhodesia.

I remember I telephoned my brother Daniel and asked him to go to the bank to get a note for me to borrow money so we could buy tickets to come home. The bank first transferred money to a credit union in South Africa, and then after six weeks, it was to be released to pay for the tickets. I said this is not going to work, so I called the bank and talked to the bank manager who was a schoolmate of mine.

I said, "Paul, can you call my brother? Ask him to come and sign another note so I can get money and deposit it into the South African Airways account in New York so it will not get lost again."

He said, "Stephen, I will lend you the money. Come in and sign the note when you arrive home."

That is what I did. He then transferred the money into the South African Airways account in New York. Our tickets were purchased.

A Bush Pastor Asks for Help

To recapture a story is not always easy. During our time of ministry in Zaire, we also experienced a multitude of miracles again and again and again. Miracles were the order of the day. Let me just relate to a few of them. In the hospital, Ruth always experienced miracles probably more in the hospital than out on the field. Although in training pastors and establishing churches, there were many, many miracles also.

All these experiences were a time of blessing. Pastors would come to pastors meeting and to teaching sessions, and they had no shoes to wear, these were average people of the bush. They did not own shoes, although they had a good heart, and that was a much greater value than shoes. If they had any kind of shoes, they were made out of tire.

But they would walk for miles, as there was no transport in the bush. To come to the meeting point where we were having at seminar. And the response was always positive. They were determined to have the blessing of God. I well remember one pastor that came to one of these meetings, and he was kindly asking for another evangelist to help him in the ministry. Our national church leader said, "We do not have enough of evangelists to put two people at one church. As we are so short of evangelist and the work is going so well, oftentimes, we would be opening a new area every month. So evangelists were very short, as we were utilizing them so rapidly."

God was faithfully confirming the Word! This requesting pastor had opened a new outreach in a very difficult area. I was not aware of the witchcraft in the area, and this made the work very difficult and spiritually hard to work with, but the pastor we placed there was a faithful child of God! And he persevered, and his church had grown to about eighty some members. And the next month when he came to the meeting, as we had meetings with pastors every month, this time, he requested more help with his ministry as he felt it was very hard. But his church was growing. And his work is going well, but he said, "No, I need more help, please help me, as the forces of hell are very strong."

The leadership did not understand what he was up against. As in this village, there was a very powerful witch doctor, one strong demon. Finally, we gave him another evangelist to help him, as his request was relentless when we gave him the second evangelist. At the next meeting were the results of help. The pastor came to the next meeting with a big smile and the witch doctor's bag and all the witch doctors medicine that he carried with him from village to village. Wow! what a revelation we had!

He then related this story to us. I was in the church. I was preaching to the people. We were having a good service when in walked this man with this bag of medicine. They did not know him. He walked right up to the front of the church, right where I was preaching. He looked right into my eyes. I did not know him. He set his bag down and raised his hand straight up. And he said these words, "I accept Jesus Christ as my Lord and Savior! Amen!"

And he got off his knees and said, "Young man, your God is more powerful than my medicine. And because of that, I accept your God as my Lord and Savior Jesus Christ. Your God is the true God. For your God is more powerful than my medicine and the god that I served.

"You were sleeping in your house, I had put my medicine in your house, but it refused to kill you. My medicine is powerful, ask any of the people here. I have killed hundreds of people with my medicine. But you would not die! Therefore, your God is more powerful than my medicine." He reached into his bag of medicine, which now the pastor was holding. He took out an animal skin and rolled up with snakes' heads inside. He unrolled the skin and the snakes' heads where sewn to this animal skin. And the snakes' heads had their tongue sticking out, that tongues were going in and out, as though they were alive. And the witch doctor said this, "This is powerful medicine, and it has killed many people. But it could not kill you. Therefore, it is no good to me." He rolled it up and put it into his bag and took out another skin.

And again, there were three snakes' heads inside the skin, and he said this, "With this medicine, I would take a baby out of this mother over here. And I would put the baby into that mother over there." Scary stuff, huh, but very powerful and very real! Now the villagers verified the truth.

Many other stories he related but sufficient to explain why he needed more help as a pastor in this village.

The joyful thing was, the witch doctor came to know Jesus Christ as Lord and Savior! And this has nothing to do with me; I was only an instrument in the battle for souls. The pastor was a real warrior. And he won the battle. Jesus died on the cross for this witch doctor, just as much as for my sin.

And again to refresh my memory, Satan is defeated, and the victory is won. Hallelujah! Jesus died at the cross, so we don't have to die. Now it is for us to trust the Word of God and to relentlessly trust him and know that his Word is truth! So we started so many churches that we could not disciple all the people, and I asked the other churches in the area if they have the ability to disciple more people in their churches, when they responded affirmative. I would then ask if they are willing to take another church of maybe 130 people and will they disciple them. So we gave away many churches that we had started because I could not disciple them all. My passion has always been souls and still is today.

To God be the glory. And may we win souls forever. My good wife, who has delivered hundreds of babies, and has now gone to be with Jesus, has been the instrument and witness of the great and mighty work of God and the Holy Ghost. She has been the instrument to bring healing to extreme and violent burns. She has sutured many violent and extreme lacerations.

I remember one time a man came in, saying come quickly and get my uncle before he dies. Usually, we did not go on an ambulance call as we did not have the extra fuel. But this time, we went to get this man. He was plowing with two oxen and a walking plow. I guess there was a lot of grass and weeds he was trying to plow under. Then he stepped on top of the weeds to get them to turn over by the plow and then become covered when he tripped his foot went down and he pushed the weeds under the plow and the point of the plow caught in the front of his foot, at the ankle, and the plow cut the front of his ankle wide open. What a gory mess. We put him into the SUV and quickly transported him to the hospital. He had just lost so much blood he was nearly unconscious. Mom then elevated his feet higher than his head to get the blood flowing into his brain so he would not collapse into unconsciousness. And then she began to suture the terrible wound. To our examination, we did not find any bones broken, so we sutured him up. And after six weeks, he went home. This is just one of the many miracles that we had seen. Mom was always calm and collected in a situation like this. She was one excellent doctor and always did an excellent job. It did not matter what kind of nasty wound. It was. Mom would sew it up with excellence and integrity, this was how Mom worked!

And another time, it was at the end of the day. Mom came from the hospital to the house and said to me, "Dad, you go up to the hospital and pray for a patient that came in. A patient has come into the hospital and is very sick. I do not know her problem, but she is extremely sick. She is so thin it almost looked as though you could see through her abdomen, only that her skin is dark." I replied. She has 2 feet in the grave already.

I went to the hospital and looked at the most sorry case I had ever seen with my eyes. As I stepped into the hospital room, she sat up in bed. She had nothing on from her waist up and what a skeleton; she was a very sorry site. I prayed for her and for the Lord to spare her life and then put her on treatment, and we treated her for two months. After two days of treatment, she said to Mom, "I have not felt so good in a long time." We gave her a very nutritious diet as she was just skin and bone. And in six weeks, she had gained 20 kg. She was only thirty-two years old and now was dying from HIV. We treated her for two months, and the test showed HIV-negative. This was our beginning to successfully treating HIV patients. What a mighty God we serve! And it is most amazing to see and to know how great our God really is! Praise the Lord, ha, hallelujah!

She then said, "I am not going to leave this place as this is where God gave me my life back." What a testimony she was for the Lord, as she told everybody that God has a plan for them and they do not have to die for their sin, as Jesus died for us and for our sin. Ha, hallelujah! What a mighty God we serve!

Cerebral Malaria

I n 1992, I was sick with malaria. I had been sick with malaria for about three weeks. I had such an excruciating headache that I said to my wife, "If this headache doesn't stop, I will need to go to South Africa for a checkup," thinking that maybe I have an injury from the accident that I had in 1969. My headache was just too much.

I remember I was sharpening saw blades and fixing tires for the Unimog, just for something to occupy my time as I had such terrible headaches. It was not a good experience for me as I had such terrible headache again and again. For about three weeks, I was on treatments for malaria. But I never thought about cerebral malaria.

Mommy had gone to the clinic that noonday and about three o'clock in the afternoon when I said, "My headache is so bad, I'm going to go lay down for a bit."

I walked to the house from the workshop, leaving Mahlon there to put all the tools away. I went and lay down in the bed in our bedroom, and I fell asleep. Mom came from the clinic at about 3:30 that afternoon. She came into the bedroom and found me lying on the bed with my head at the foot end. She tried to wake me, but I would not respond. She shook my body to wake me up, but I would not respond, come to find that I had lapse into a coma.

She called for Mahlon to come and help her. They turned my body around and put me properly in bed. She then went to the container to get some serum drips, or IV. She then started an IV on me, as I was unconscious. She was treating malaria every day, and she has had a lot of experience. Mommy had treated many cerebral malaria cases, but this time, it was her husband, and that made it extremely serious. She then treated me with injectable quinine. This was the ultimate treatment and the only treatment that we were using at that time. She had me on an IV drip we had just received from South Africa when we were there, which they gave to us with reluctance. They said they have helped many missionaries and they have taken advantage of the treatment, but they said they will help us this one time.

All night, I was treated with quinine and with IV. It was a tedious job. I was not a well-behaved patient. I pulled the IV needle out of my arm a number of times as it irritated me. So you see, I did not behave myself well. Nevertheless, I was being treated. I was now being watched on an hourly basis. It was challenging as I was in a coma. For Mother, at this time, it was very difficult to know it was her husband, her dearly beloved husband, and as he was not responding. That made the situation all the more very intense, but there was no time to relent.

Much prayer went up on behalf of Dad who was in a coma. Mom and Mahlon looked after me as I was in intensive care. They watched me very closely. We had a ham radio for communication. Mahlon got on the radio and talked to the doctors, concerning my illness and the treatment. And the doctor suggested we come immediately to receive treatment as he was not aware we were in another country and in the bush and that many miles away from this doctor as he was in Northeast America. Mahlon suggested that maybe they should overdose with quinine, but the doctors suggested that you do not want to overdose with quinine as it had side effects and quinine lowers blood sugar and that is not good in this case. But after the third day, I was still not responding. Mahlon again had a conversation with the doctor in Zimbabwe. Again, he asked about the possibility of overdosing with quinine, and the doctor again said no. It was then when he said, "We treat malaria on a daily basis and what we know is, if you do not arrest malaria, it will arrest you." The doctor said, "You have to be very careful, and you do not want to overdose with quinine."

Mahlon then said, "It is my dad that is in a coma, and he is not responding to treatment. We are going to overdose." What we have learned is, if you don't arrest malaria it will arrest you.

He then mixed quinine himself, being a pharmaceutical technician. He made a dosage 50% stronger, and they applied it to me in the IV. Just a few hours later, I began to respond. The treatment now was successful, and there was great joy in the land. Everyone was so happy. I regained consciousness on day four. Dad who has been lying here for four days was now beginning to move for the first time in four days.

God is so amazing and so precious. Everyone was so delighted and happy. Oh the amazing jealousy of God. Joy was now in abundance. Dad was once again opening his eyes, and he showed signs of recovery.

The last four days were trials and tribulations, but now I was beginning to respond. There was great joy in the house. On an hourly basis day and night, Mom and Mahlon took their turn caring for Dad. I showed signs of recovery! Praise the Lord! As I was slowly showing signs of life, even though I was still in a coma, Mom said she was still able to give me some of my mint tea. I was a great lover of mint tea. Mom wanted to get some tea into me with a spoon, and she put it in my mouth. I was still able to swallow. All during my coma, she was able to give me some mint again. In the last three weeks or so, I had lost about twenty-five pounds. I looked very thin, and I was still not eating solid food. As I was lying there in bed, Mahlon said to me, "Dad, you're looking at the ceiling as though you are watching a TV screen. What do you see?"

I answered him, "Over here on the right side is so and so." I would name the person I was seeing. "Over here is this one," and I mention his name. "Then over here is this one," and I mention his name.

He said, "But who are these people that you are seeing?"

I replied, "They are old historians. I see this one over here." Then I went between the layers of soil and then between the water. I went over here to this one, and I love visiting with him. Then I traveled over to this side and saw this one. Then I went beyond all this, and I visited with Smith Wigglesworth, and I was visiting with him. He was sitting in his English home, in his living room with a kerosene light on the table. I talked with him for some time, but I do not remember what we talked about. He was sitting at the end of the table with his three-piece suit on. We had a wonderful conversation, but I do not remember what we were talking about. It was then when he said, "Dad, are you aware of that you were having an out of the body experience? What you are telling me is that you have been moving through the elements of the earth. You have been visiting with Smith Wigglesworth. I know he was your favorite pentecostal hero, but he died I think in 1941. If you had a visit with him, then for sure you had an experience out of the physical body. These people that you have been seeing are also people that have died many years ago, so for sure you are telling us strange things."

Then day by day, I began to improve. I began to eat a little food again. But improvement was very slow as I still had malaria in my body. I remember one forenoon as I was lying in bed, still very weak, I was beginning to develop an appetite. Someone from the village had stopped by the house. He had a back leg of a big porcupine. He said, "Do you want to buy this meat as the local people ate everything that moves?"

Mom said, "No, I am not interested in porcupine meat."

I had started to develop an appetite, and I was hungry. I said, "Come on, bring it here, I want to see it. How much is it? I want to buy it, I am hungry."

Mom bought it and cooked it. That was the first meat I had after I had come out of the coma. Praise the Lord! It tasted very good to me! I enjoyed every bit of it, but I was still a long way from being well. I recovered very slowly. I remember when I first started to get up and walk around, I was so weak, and Mom helped me to walk to the other end of the living room. Then I was tired, and I returned to bed. Little by little, I began to walk again, but progress was slow. I was determined so again and again, and I tried to walk. Yes, I was so weak, but the more I ate, the better I felt, of course, because the body uses fat cells. When you take food, that is how you get fat cells for your body, how clever I must be, lol!

Progress was very, very slow, and it took a long time for me to completely recover. My body was on the mend even though I was still full of malaria but did not know it. Little by little, I was gaining my strength back, but I was not fully recovered, and I was still very, very thin. I looked like a POW, someone that has not eaten for a long time.

After a given period of time, Mom said, "Dad is not getting well. We are in the bush 250 miles away from Lubumbashi. It is the month of September, and it is still the dry season. Let's pack our things and go to South Africa and take Dad to get checked."

It has been too long with that being his condition. It is five weeks since he came out of the coma. "Mahlon and Becky, go and pack your things. I'm getting things ready to leave tomorrow. I will pack a suitcase for Dad and myself. We will put a mattress in the back of the pickup, and we will drive to South Africa where we can get treatment for Dad."

Early the next morning, we got everyone loaded in the pickup, and we left, driving slowly. I was on a mattress in the back of the old 1979 Land Cruiser. I do not remember where we spent the night in Lubumbashi, but we made it all right. We were on our journey the next four or five days, as we had to travel nearly two thousand miles. The first night we spent in Zambia was with Rob Sheal and his good wife Urshela. I do not remember, but maybe we spent two nights there. Then we went to see Anita at school. She was being educated at Chengelo Secondary School in Mukushi, Zambia. I remember when we drove into school and Anita's friends shouted, "Anita, your parents are here." She came running. What a surprise that we had arrived. She went and saw Mom climb out of the cab of the Land Cruiser, Mahlon and his wife also, but no Dad. She thought I must be napping in the back, so she ran to the back. I climbed out of the back of the Land Cruiser. She was ready to fling herself into my arms, as we had a very close relationship.

Mahlon said, "Look at Dad." She started to run, but Mahon grabbed her. He said, "Look at him," then she realized how frail I was.

She started to cry and said, "What is wrong with Dad?"

Mom said, "He has nearly died from malaria. He was in a coma four days, and now we are on our way to South Africa for Dad to get treatment."

We had a good visit, and then we spent the night at Barton Young's. We then left early the next day, and we traveled to Lusaka and spent the night with Helmuth Reutter. We left early the next morning on our way to the Chirundu Border. There we crossed into Zimbabwe and headed south to Harare and arrived at Voysey's late in the afternoon. They were very special and dear friends of ours we have met a long time ago. We met this precious couple during the war in 1978 when we lived in Harare. At that time, it was still called Salisbury, Rhodesia.

The next day, we left as we were desperate to reach South Africa. So we drove to Masovingo and stayed with Willy and Cory Landsberg. They were people that we had met back in 1988 when I was coming through with the truck and it broke down there. Now again, we stopped there for the night. They were a special spirit-filled couple who always had room for us when we came passing through. This time, of course, it was very different since I was so ill with malaria. When we finished there, the next morning, we left for Petersburg, South Africa. In South Africa, we went to stay with Dennis Ball. They also were folks we had met in South Africa at Rhema Bible Training Center. We spend the night with them before as they lived right on the main road. After that, we drove on to brother Harry's place in Pietersburg, Piet. There we also stayed one night. I remember brother Harry said to Mahlon, "Your father looks like a POW. For sure I will never see him again since he was so sick." Then we drove to Johannesburg and went to the city hospital. We arrived there about six o'clock in the evening, but we did not have the money they were asking for, and therefore, they refused to treat me. They would not have us. They refused to treat me. So we left, and I think we went to Ken's place. I do not remember where we stayed. Maybe we went to Hands of Compassion as we were good friends with them too.

The next morning, they took us to the tropical disease hospital in Reit Fontaine. There they admitted me, and they began to look at my situation. I had a very good Jewish doctor, and he cared for me very much. They examined my blood and found that it was still full of malaria. They put me on quinine and treated me for eight days.

After six days, there was no more malaria in my blood. But they had some questions to ask me before I was discharged. They said they wanted to take one day to interview me. They said, "We have checked your heart, we have checked your kidneys, your bladder, and your spleen. We can find no gunge in your system whatsoever. For sure you eat no sugar or any salt, as you have no build up in your arteries at all."

Then Mom said, "But he inhales salt and sugar."

"Why have you been in a coma for four days and have no physical collapse as such. We can show you any amount of people that have been in a coma for one day or even a half day and some for three days. All these have physical breakdown. Some are as a person that had a stroke with half of their body physically paralyzed. Some have a thrombosis and had to have heart surgery. Some have kidney failure and are on a dialysis, and some have a liver collapse. But you have none of these and no signs of these. Why are you different?"

They grilled me for a long time. They flew in thirty-six of their top malaria specialists from all over south Africa for this interview. They grilled me, and they would not relent.

I said, "I don't know. What are you after?"

They said, "We are after the reason why you are still alive. Any normal person would have died from a four-day coma. This illness is a killer, and we cannot find why your system is so clean."

For two and a half hours, they grilled me to try and find out what it is that has made my system so clean. They asked me what I drink, what I don't drink, what I eat, and what I do not eat. I said, "I eat anything, and the first foods I ate when I came out of the coma was porcupine."

They then laughed, but they grilled me for some time. Then they said, "Do you drink tea?"

"Yes, I drink tea."

"Do you drink hot tea?"

"Yes, I drink hot tea."

"Do you drink Roibous, a herbal tea from South Africa?"

"Yes, I drink this tea but not that often as it is not available in Zaire."

"Understood. Then what kind of tea do you drink?"

"I drink a mint."

"Mint, what is that? I have never heard of drinking mint. What kind of tea is that?"

I explained, "The same plant that you make your mint sauce from when you have mutton."

He said, "We don't drink that."

I said, "I do! I like mint, so I drink often two cups after each meal."

"How long have you been drinking this stuff?"

"Maybe fifteen years." I like it, so I drink it."

Then the old man chairing the meeting, a seventy-four-year-old doctor, said this, "Let us stop right here. Listen what this man is saying. We need to hear this. He is saying he has been drinking mint tea, hot tea, and he has no build up in his system at all. That speaks volumes to me. I am a doctor. I am a specialist in abdominal care. This man is saying he has been drinking this tea for fifteen years. Therefore, he is saying something that we need to hear. He is a healthy man, but he is sick with malaria. He had been in a four-day coma, but he has no physical collapse whatsoever. He will never have a heart attack or kidney stones or gallstones, his system is clean. Why? Because mint is a cleanser and a purifier. Therefore, he has no physical buildup in his system." He turned to me, and he said, "This is what we are looking for. This is why you survived. The interview is finished. Now you will be discharged, and you will be able to go home. We have learned a multitude of things just from you. Thank you very much. We have treated you for malaria, and I have cared for you at my own expense because you have taught us so much. Thank you so much, and God bless you. You are now discharged, and you can go home."

So we left the hospital, and we went to stay with the parents of Pastor Jaques. They had immigrated there from Switzerland, and God blessed them in business. And we stayed with them for five weeks as I recovered.

And now we had become good friends with these precious people. I had regained my strength as now I think it was February and we were ready to go back to Zaire. I remember while we were at hands of compassion and we had the transmission out of the Land Cruiser to put a new rear seal in the gearbox. And Ursula McHuew said, "You people must be real missionaries as you always are busy at work, and we always see you again and again and fixing what needs to be fixed, so you can get on with your work in the bush." So finally, it was time to go back. We said goodbye to everyone, and we begin to travel on our way home. Again on the way, we stopped with friends every night. We have learned over the years the value of friends. They all lived along the two thousand miles, we had to travel, as we traveled toward Zambia and then Zaire, passing through Zimbabwe. At this point in time, South Africa and Zimbabwe had very good roads. But then Zambia had deteriorated so much, it took us all day to drive to Chingola, as there were potholes everywhere. After spending our last days with Shiels, we left Chingola and drove to Lubumbashi. We spent one night in the guesthouse and then proceeded to drive home. It was now the middle of rainy season and the roads were horrendously bad. All the way home was mud, mud, and more mud. I think it took us three days to arrive home. Every bridge had to be fixed so we can get through. It was a tremendous challenge. But this was our way of life in Zaire. After we left Kasomana, we headed due north with one ton of supplies in the Land Cruiser and one ton in the trailer. And we could not drive fast as the roads were so bad. When we came to the first big village, the people all came running out, and they danced around the vehicle. They acted as though they were having a wild party and as what they would do if it was the president.

I said, "These people are crazy, why are they acting like this." When we are returning, at this point, I was at the wheel. So finally, we got through the maze, and we headed for the next village with so much mud and potholes. Mud and potholes were saying it vaguely, after dark that evening we came to a large swimming pool size pothole. Now when we drove through the swimming pool mudhole, the Land Cruiser could not pull the trailer out of the pothole, and I did not have any long chains along and no cable, only a short chain and the come-along. So we got the trailer unhooked, and then the Land Cruiser could go forward to where it was on solid road, but now how are we to get the trailer out? I had a good 12 V. spotlight. I got it out and stood on top of the Land Cruiser and looked if there was anywhere a tree that had a branch about twenty feet long so I can put it between the Land Cruiser and the trailer. Now the grass was very long, and there were no trees near the road. At about two hundred feet through the tall grass, there was one tree with a long branch that I thought will do the job. So we took the chain saw. Becky stood on top of Land Cruiser with a spotlight and shown down to that tree. And three of us started wadding through the tall grass toward the tree. I am sure as we passed through the grass. There were plenty of snakes, but they now had to find someplace else to go as we the children of God were now on a mission. And we trudged forward toward this tree. When we reached the tree, we cut down the tree and then cut that branch about twenty feet long at the small end. It was about three inches thick in diameter. And the other end was about eight inches. Now how are we going to get it out to the road?

So we looked at the tree, and Mahlon said, "If you can take that heavy *end* of this branch and help me to lift it onto my shoulder, I will carry the heavy end, and you two people can carry the other end as I was not so strong as yet." So we put that heavy end of the branch on his shoulder, we picked up the other end, and Kafwimbe and I carried the other end when we were halfway to the road. We had to stop and rest, as it was difficult walking through that tall grass. When we got to the road, Mahlon said, "Do not stop but go slowly as the mud is very slippery." We had to walk through the one large pothole. Mahlon held on tightly, and his feet slipped down into the pothole, but he held on to the branch then walked through the water to the trailer. Then we laid down our end and took the other end off his shoulder and laid it down. Then we tied the short chain on to the trailer hitch, and with the come-along, we put the other end fastened to the Land Cruiser and then pulled the trailer right out. So it was all this hour and one half of work to get the trailer out. And now Mahlon had to change clothes as he was wet. So we drove to the next village and bunked down for the night.

When we got up the next morning, all the villagers were happy to see us. So we got fresh mangoes and drove to the nearby river where we washed and cleaned up and then had a good breakfast which we had a long from South Africa. Yes, the journey, it was tiresome, but now we were nearly at home just about 180 km more. At the bridge, there was plenty of water from the river. So we washed, felt refreshed, and we journeyed onward. Yes, we got stuck many times. Finally, we reached the top of the mountain, and we were 30 km from home. So what is usual is that there are always trees down across the road, many places along the way. So we had to cut away six trees on our way home just on top of the mountain.

As we came to the larger villages, they all performed as they did in the first one. Three villages we passed through with the same performance, I said, "What on earth is possessing these people to act like this." Then I began to listen to what they are saying.

And they were singing and chanting saying, "You see, you see, the God of the missionary is greater than the god of the witch doctor. And this is why they had such a performance."

When we left to go to South Africa, the witch doctors said, "The missionaries are now gone, and they will never come back. And now they have come back and Mr. Fisher is driving, and the God of the missionary is the great God. And the god of the witch doctor is only speaking lies. We will follow the God of the missionaries!"

So we started to rejoice with them and then drove on home. Amazing, our God is an awesome God! Hallelujah, and thank you, Jesus!

God's Vindication at Kashiobwe

s soon as bricks were made, we wanted to start to put up new buildings. Now we were living up in the mountains. And at night, it was very cold, and in the early morning coming to work to make bricks was no man's desire, as the mud that had to be mixed and was done by walking around in the mud. And it was ice cold. And there were only two boys that they would do that early in the morning. The others were not interested because it was so cold. But Ngala and Chicholacoso were the only two men who would tramp the mud first thing in the morning because they got cold feet. But these two men did a good job, and they used to do this first thing in the morning to make some mud for the bricks. Then we would put this mud into brick molds. As measured eight inches wide, and six inches deep, and ten inches long, the bricks were very heavy. But in those days, they only built our muscles. And the building went up very fast as with this brick, it covered a lot of territory. So we began to do our building after we've made bricks. But first, to make bricks, we lay them out on the ground to dry then stack them into a kiln and bake them with fire and then burn whole trees in the kiln. Yes, it is a lot of hard work, but then we had a good brick to build the mission. At my age, I would find an easier way not because it would not be a good way, but I cannot work like that now, and now we have a brick machine. So the fact being was that we only had a short dry season, three months in total. And we had to have all the bricks made and burned. Boy, did we work! And the blessing of God was with us; somehow, we always have food. And the work flourished. During the time when we were making bricks, we also had built a temporary clinic. Mom was busy every day in the clinic. This was Mom's place. And it was her chosen profession. And it's where she exceled. All kinds of illnesses came to the clinic: lacerations, burned bodies, and—most of all—malaria. Malaria was the biggest killer of them all. But Mother never complained as she minister to these needs. She puts up with a lot of inconveniences, as she did not have things convenient. And she worked very hard eight hours a day in the clinic. Frequently, we would come with cut fingers. With a grateful heart, she would continue to work and minister to people, with all kind of the illnesses, then this little girl is brought in by a wheelbarrow ambulance, she had a broken femur in her right leg. You did not have many broken bones, but there were some. So while Mom was looking after the afflicted and the sick and the needy people, we were beginning to lay the foundations of the buildings now in a new place and a new area in the mountains. It was gorgeously beautiful.

So about five times a year, we would go to South Africa to get supplies. I had to stop in Zimbabwe. As we have friends that had a business of repairing microscopes, the gentleman that fixed the microscopes and said he knew a man in town who sold dumpy levels, so I went to him and asked him how much I have to pay for a dumpy level. I think if I remember correctly I paid $125 for it. It was a surveyor's level that was used on the mines. It was a very good and precision machine. One time, it had cost a lot of money. So I bought it and used it for building my buildings. With it, I made straight roads. And I leveled up my buildings. It was a beautiful piece of technology. It was such an instrument of blessing. With this instrument, I would also make right angles. It was such a special machine. And so we began to put in the foundations of the building. And walls on the buildings began to rise. Progress was on the way, summertime had come out again. And now making bricks was not so cold. We worked very hard as we constructed the building. We had to haul all our bricks with the Unimog. We worked long hard days.

And another missionary family had arrived with their son and their daughter and the mother-in-law. I was only introduced to Mother and Father. And I was not aware of the rest of the family, and she was a divorced lady who I was not aware that she was in the picture. The son was fourteen years old, the daughter was thirteen years old, and they all came at the same time. The daughter lived with her grandmother in one tent while the father and mother lived in their own tent. And the son and Mahlon slept in the upstairs of the trailer that we have brought from South Africa.

While mother and I slept in the storeroom I had built, I had built a storage unit as of just putting poles in the ground and tying them together at the top. Then we put a roof over top of that, and that was our storage room. We had put about twenty drums in there. We then put our mattresses on top of the drums, and that was our bed we lived like this for maybe six months until we had built the small house. At the same time, we were busy building this house, our small house. We were also busy building the first larger house with three bedrooms that we were building for the new family. However by the time, we had built a house for them. They were already unhappy and were moving out. We had such problems with those precious people. They just seem to never settling to what we are doing, they had an agenda of their own, I don't even like to record this aspect of the journey as it was not nice. But it is the true fact and life. They were special people. Mom had trained the wife to help her in the clinic. But there was forever an undercurrent with the wife's mother. And I think she was the problem of the whole situation. I did not know she was coming, as I was only introduced to the father and mother. Anyway, we fought the good fight. There are many things that transpired, please forgive me, but do not ask me to relive those days. They were not good. And it so poisoned the church at the time that the church had to see for themselves the truth of the matter. Finally, the people came through as they understood this truth. But it was a long hard process. Situations like this we have found that occur many times in mission life. It is heart rendering and painful. And I do not understand why we had to experience this, except to tell others to beware of evildoers. This is a hard thing to learn. Jesus experienced this, and so did all the apostles. There are always situations, so very necessary, in the procedure of life. But we are working with human beings, and that is the way man is! And it seemed they were going to the ends of the earth to destroy us. All I can say is that God was not finish with us yet and that God was turning a page in our life, printing a new page and fortifying our Spirit so that we would better be able to stand against the wiles of the devil. They had written a letter to the leadership of the church. While still working with us in Zaire, every mission group had to be identified with the government and had to be recognized by government. Then the government gave everyone an identification number for their organization.

They wrote a letter to the government headquarters. They had five major statements listed as to why they disapproved of us in our work. Headquarters believed their story without ever investigating us. So headquarters wrote back and disqualified us and asked us to leave the country. While we still lived at Kashiobwe. One day, a military officer got off the boat and came to visit us. So he came to me as he had heard that there were new American missionaries that had just arrived. He spoke a good English, where in Zaire, the national language was French, and he greeted me as Mr. Fisher. And he was speaking a very good English. And I said to him, "My friend, where are you from? You speak a very good English."

He said, "Yes, I learned when I was in school in Texas. I am in the military. And I did my ballistic missile training in Texas. I was there for eight months."

We had developed a close relationship as he too was from the Presbyterian Church and became a very good friend of ours. Many times when we went to town, we would stop at his village and even have a meal at his house. We were one of the family until the day that we left the country. His name was Adjacent Chief Kalala, a high-ranking military officer. He loved the Lord, and he was our good friend. So when all this palava came up and now the church covering disowned us, then the government would not support you either, and normally, you would have to leave the country. This is what this family had hoped would happen, and nearly, it did. But they had not consulted our God. For God had another plan.

October 17

Now at the mission, we were still busy building as we were in a race against the rainy season that was coming. So we were very busy.

But now we got this letter from the church headquarters. It said they no longer were going to support us. And we knew that that means we have to leave the country. They had already been into town and spoke lies everywhere. And most missionaries believe them. So the damage was done. But God had not died, but I think I can say we were startled, wondering what we have done that has caused this rift, as all five accusations were lies. And they contained no truth. Now in this state, what is our defense? So we have to go to town before the government comes and throws us out of their country. So we drove to Lubumbashi. Every missionary, we met smirked at us. And we knew we were unwelcome. Hard times, I wanted to cry, no one wanted to hear my story. It just wasn't fair, but it was not a situation of fairness. It was a situation where God has to come through, or we are finished. So I went to see this military officer. He was the only official that I had a closer relationship with during this mess. He said, "Mr. Fisher, let us take your vehicle, and you drive us to the military headquarters of this province at Kapushi, a town to the south."

The next day, we went to see the top military officer in the province. I do not really remember his name, he only greeted me as a foreigner. And then chef unraveled his story. He reached out to me and asked me for the letter. He looked at the letter. He said, "Who is this church? I am not familiar with this church." And he looked straight in my face.

"I shall never forget his look—a look of anger and discuss—not to me but the church."

He said, "Who is this church? I do not know them but Mr. Fisher." Now there was a smile on his face. He said, "I know who you are, you live at Kashiobwe, you arrived there in 1982. You planted three churches in the village. You restored the old hospital there and have done a big medical work. I know who you are. But this church, who are they? I do not know them. Five things they have spoken against you, and all five are lies. And then they want you to leave this country. I am the only official in this country that can ask you to leave. Mr. Fisher, do you understand? No man can throw you out of this country except me. And I am qualifying the work that you're doing for the work that you have done makes a sure qualification valid. So be at peace, no one can throw you out of this country."

I began to cry. As for me at this point of time, it was a bit overwhelming. For we were nearly shaking in their boots, knowing that God called us and that there was a big work to do, and Mom was so busy with the hospital work. But now Satan was causing havoc.

"Well, my friend, what else does Satan have left to do? He is a liar. Jesus said he is the father of lies, so what can we expect!"

Oh, let man declare this day, stand up and be counted, for Jesus Christ is Lord of lord, and forever will be King of kings! Hallelujah! So being joyfully overwhelmed, we left that small city. Chef Kalala was with us. He said, "You see, these people did not consider God, and so they have failed. So now what you do, you go back home, pick up the pieces, and keep on moving forward and finish the project that you have started."

When we arrived back at the mission, these dear friends had already started to do their own thing. They told all the villagers in the whole area, that we were never coming back, and that they are here to stay and they are going to take over the work. Now we returned, and we took over as usual, much of the work we had to do by ourselves, as no one wanted to help us. They had given many gifts to the people who had nothing, who were not able to buy salt and sugar except that from the mission store. They literally gave fifty pounds of sugar and fifty pounds of salt, clothing and shoes, and pots and pans. And whatever they could to bribe the people and to win their favor, they did a good job of it. So after about one week going by, no one wanted to help us to build the new mission, except one boy had come. He was the son of a prostitute. And he was not easily swayed by the smooth talk of these people. His name was Kalenga. And he came and helped us. And we talked to him about that we need more help. So that evening when he went home from work, he did something on his own. He went to talk to the chief. The chief by this time had made a commitment to Jesus Christ. And he was very happy with the work that we were doing. So the chief called a community meeting. And he explained to the people how that these traitors that came to work with us were telling them lies about us and that he had given this land to us and not to these other people and said they were not going to take over. He set everyone straight on the situation. I never could have accomplished this without the chief's help, and I think at this time. This great problem was behind us. And from that time on, we went forward.

He told the chief, "No one wants to come to work for us."

So the chief came the next day and talked to the people and said, "These people had left and taking their possessions." And they went away and left us in perfect peace, and we experienced the tremendous blessing of God, and we returned to build a new mission that we had started, and we didn't even finished the house at that time, as when these folk left, they left their dirty trace follow only for a short time. As they were soon forgotten, the chief was a staunch supporter. So when the local people refused to show up to work, the chief talked to them and told them those people were traitors and they were not good people and that they should support the work that we are doing. It may be that it took one month until the lies had turned sour. And the reality of the truth was revealed. And we were up and running again. It was just a long sad story. But praise the lord, we have learned through it, and we shall prosper forever because of it.

Jesus said, "If you do not forgive those who trespass against you, neither will your heavenly father forgive you" (Matt. 6:15). The church also was much stronger. And God did many great miracles in our midst all the time. I don't remember which building we built next. First, the small house, then the big house, then we had left the big house for a time as these people had left. I think next we build the hospital. That was a big necessary accomplishment.

The first building we worked on was the workshop and the big storeroom with the office on top of the workshop on the second floor. The work was going forward, and the rain had come. I remember we had to work very hard to get buildings finished before the rain set in. And we could not get cement at the time, so we were using anthill dirt which was also a very solid material to work with in place of cement. It worked well, it just did not dry as fast. And we had to hurry as we were putting on a grass roof as tin roofing. It was very expensive, so we completed the workshop and office with grass roof.

Then we placed tin roof over the outside of the workshop. The whole storeroom also had tin roof which we did not have the money for tin over the office area, so that is why we did the office in grass. Grass is also more delightful, it is cooler in the summertime, and it is warmer in the wintertime. And this grass roof was there thirteen years and still was in very good shape. So there is nothing wrong with a grass roof, you just cannot have it under a tree where a tree will be weeping water on it as a constant drip of water on the roof will root the grass. So that covered my office space and then workshop. On the side of the workshop was a tin roof, which acted as a porch next to the workshop as an extra workshop space, the whole storage area, and then this was our storeroom. The whole storeroom I had built with broken bricks that were not used for building the house. The storeroom walls were about seven feet high with a flat roof on top. And it served its purpose well. I remember we used to have such a terrible problem in the storeroom with rats. It was a dirt floor, and the rats dug holes everywhere. And many times, we found a snake in the storeroom as they were busy catching rats, and I was okay with that as not all snakes are enemies. But sometimes, it was a spitting cobra. And that is not okay, and they also have a venomous bite. Rat poison we could not get, so I made my own. I took the gas sulfur tablets that we used to kill insects in corn and beans and whatever these weevils would get into, this one particular gas tablet we would use to treat corn. So I said, "If it kills weevils, maybe it will kill rats." So I remember going to experiment with the anything for everything. So I took three gas tablets, and crush them to powder, and put it into cornflower that we used to use to make porridge. Wow, to my amazement, I mixed it into the meal, and the next morning, there were no rats at all. There were no rats running anywhere, only a sound of rats croaking. They were coughing, they were growling, but no rats anywhere. They were all gone—unbelievable. It really works. And so we graciously got rid of the rat population. I know we know how to get rid of rats now.

So after, we had the workshop built, the bedroom for Mom, and I was in the office area as we did not yet have our house built. So we moved from our tent to the office as the storeroom was finished, then Mahlon's bedroom was upstairs where Mom and I were sleeping in the room which was known as my office, but it was also a bedroom. And if guests came, they would sleep there also. It was a bit crammed, but it would offer a good night sleep. And that office was where all our technical electric electronic work was done. I had a small gas soldering irons there. And all our electrical fittings were done in this office. I had put a stairway going up to the office. It was a different kind of building for the bush, as two-story buildings were not found there. Next, we started to build the hospital. That structure and building was much greater. It was about this time the medical work had grown into a huge work. Mom was an excellent doctor. She had a lot of experience. She was such a beautiful person. Patients would come from all the way across the mountain. Some said they walked three days to get there. They would always bring a gift for the medicine. Most of all, our medical work was done on the barter system. They would bring a bag of beans, or a half a bag of corn, or a chicken or a goat in payment for the medicine, for they have no money to pay for medicine. Money was inflating so fast in Zaire. No one could put a price on things with money. So it was much more reliable through payment with animals, or chicken, or with food to eat. So the work continued to grow, and we completed the hospital. In one year during this time of hospital work, Mama was doing a lot of deliveries. Many people came to the hospital to give birth to a child. Mom was known very well as someone to deliver the baby. The other big things that you had on the daily basis was malaria—more malaria cases. We were still very busy developing the mission. However in 1990, I got the sawmill. I have been looking at a sawmill because that is what we need to do our building. Many people showed me portable sawmills. And I began to look around when we arrived in America. Many different brand names we looked at. Then one time when I was at Indianapolis, someone took me to Woodmizer Sawmill Factory. I talked to the president of the company. As he sat down and had lunch with me, his parents came here as Polish refugees and what a beautiful brother he was. We talked for some time. Then he said we would qualify to get one as a gift. But he said their gifts were given through an organization from California. So I flew to California to talk to this organization's office. But they refused to recognize me as a viable mission. I do not know what their problem was. But they would not donate me a mill. It is a long story. But they would not give me a mill. So I returned to the office and Indianapolis. And again, I talked with the president. He was grossly annoyed. And he said this, "I have had enough of complaints about this organization. Therefore, we will not again give that organization another mill as we have complaints about their administration. But for you, Mr. Fisher, you qualified to have a free mill donated to you, and since they refuse to give you a sawmill to use for your mission work, they will get no more donations from us. But since you qualify, I will personally donate a sawmill to you and your organization."

So he donated one to us—Project Redemption Ministries, an LT 40 sawmill—and we made plans to have it transported via container to Zaire. It was hard times in Zaire. But God made a way for us to do a great work, and when the container reached Zaire, they unloaded everything and put it in the state warehouse. And that was where we picked up the goods from. But then they stole my container, loaded with copper, and sent it to South Africa to the port. But I lost the container. Such is life in the bush. But they decided to retrieve my shipment, including the sawmill, praise the lord! And the sawmill was such a tremendous instrument of blessing. As we cut timber and made a number of big things for the hospital and the home, Zaire had about ten different kinds of hardwood and gorgeously beautiful—blood red wood with black grain. It was nice it was beautiful, and we made many beautiful things out of wood. I made one huge picnic table out of a tree that was lying on the ground and was dried and well seasoned. It was 4.8 m long that was nearly a 14 foot table, again gorgeously beautiful and extremely heavy. So much so that six people could not carry it. And then we built a new mission up on top of a huge hill. It was a very beautiful area up in the mountains. When we looked to the west of this location, we would see beautiful waterfalls. That was just a beautiful location. There we started to build a new mission. I cut posts twenty-one feet long and planting them four feet into the ground. If I remember correctly, I have planned eighteen of these posts, thirty-six feet of this long building on the first floor, what is for the living quarters. Underneath was for storage. On the end of the building was for storing the vehicles and workshop. If we could have finished it, it would have been one beautiful structure. All the material was cut out by this sawmill. It was a fourteen horse gas engine. But still it is a beautiful job. I talked to the manufacture of the sawmill and asked, "Why they don't have a diesel engine on the sawmill?" I kept pestering them about a diesel motor for the sawmill as gas was so expensive and hard to get. Finally, they began to build them with diesel motors on them. And what an improvement this was. When the war came and swept us out of the country, we already had our new mission building. About half completed roof was on half of the building, and the main structure was half constructed. So we were making good progress. I remember when I went to buy the iron sheets and we went to pay for $1,500 worth of roofing material. I went to the bank to get the money. At that time, they had printed money notes worth five million in one note, as the money had devaluated so much. My friend reversed his Mercedes-Benz up to the door of the bank. And we had four suitcases full of money, and many more boxes filled with bills, and it filled up his trunk and the back seat of the car, and we drove to the merchant. And we began to count the money. It took so many bills that it took us two hours and forty-five minutes to count the money. Only later that evening, when we were finished counting the money, did we then load up the roofing sheets and drive to the guesthouse parking lot, which was walled in an area that was supposed to be safe. Such were the early days of Zaire.

This was 1996. Now I am told things are very different today. I would love to go back and see the place today. But I was held hostage there for ten days, and the church has asked me to not return, as they fear for my life. As a young man who was growing up in the village of Kashiobwe, when we arrived there in 1982, he was fifteen years old and grew up in that village. He has today become governor of the city of Lubumbashi and governor of the entire province of Katanga and will probably be the next president of the country. The existing government has caused him to go into exile for his own safety. When we reached the village of Kashiobwe, he was fifteen years old, and our son was eighteen years old, and the two were good friends together at that time. His name is Moses Katumbe. His father was a Jew from Italy. And his mother was a local Bemba woman from that village. Moses seemed to be one of the most intelligent children of the family. I also knew other brothers and sisters of Moses. And they were just like other normal villagers. But Moses was very clever and intelligent, and he grew up to be a sharp businessman. And he did very well in business and became very wealthy. He was a hard-working young man, grew up in the Catholic faith, and he had many friends and was a friend of ours during those days. He even wanted to marry my daughter. So she was much younger than him. He was a friend of the family.

Now we took the roof sheets to Nsonga and began to put on the new building. This was the roof sheets that we paid so many bills for a whole Mercedes-Benz trunk full plus boxes in the back seat, this expensive roofing for our building, that took two and a half hours to count all the money. That is how useless the currency has become. They gave as much in five million notes as possible, and the rest was given in smaller notes, and that's why it took forever to count it. I hope America will never have to get to be in a situation like this, but we have lived it in Zaire, again in Zambia, and now today also in Zimbabwe.

So count your blessings, my dear friends, because I see the handwriting on the wall. We have been there, and we have done that. I do not ask anyone to experience what we have experienced. So now we were in the process of building a new mission on top of the mountain ridge. I have great dreams for their area. Inside Zaire, there were lakes and rivers everywhere. As I looked down from the high mountain ranges, there was a river flowing through the valley. At the far end of the valley, there were two mountain ranges coming right out to where the river flowed through. I looked at the valley over to the left, there was a waterfall coming down from the mountain range. There was another river flowing over into the valley and where the river left this area, it was an ideal place to build a dam. And being a dreamer, I said, I would like to dam the river with those two mountain ranges come together. It was only about two hundred feet wide. And it would have backed up a huge dam, an excellent ideal place for hydroelectric. Yes, I am a dreamer, if I can make life better for people in a situation. That is my passion. So on top of this high mountain range, we were now constructing a new mission. We did not know that it was going to be short-lived. We worked very hard, and construction was very beautiful. But in 1996, it all came to an abrupt end, as another war broke out in the country and a rebel leader that was a Muslim came and fought again the existing military government and brought this government to an end. And he took over the country. It is a long story, but I will try to recapture it and tell you the story the best that I can.

Aaron Ressler
A Special Volunteer

Now a bit of time had passed, some months have gone by, and Anita—our daughter, who was born in Africa—she grew up and was educated in Africa. She had finished school, and she came to me the beginning of 1996, and she said, "Daddy, I have been in Africa all my life. And I do not know the youth group of my own home church in America. Would you allow me to go to America now and learn to know my youth group, as I would like to grow up as someone that knows America?" It was a bit traumatic. But we agreed. And so Ruth chose to go to America with her and introduce her to a new way of life. And so soon, arrangements were made for her to fly to America with Mom and be introduced to a new cultural way of life. It was not easy, and it had many conflicts. But speaking from hindsight, she has made it with flying colors. She is my daughter, and I love her very much, as do most of the people that know her. She is special, I love her so much. They ended up staying in America for some time. I think they left in February 1996 and stayed for some months. Mom needed to get a job, and Mom began to work in a nursing home to occupy her time in America. Anita then bought a car for herself that turned out to be a problem. And Mom bought a '79 Ford. And it served everybody very well.

During this time in Africa, Aaron Rissler had been with us for nearly two years. He had come as a volunteer to work with us for one year, but he caught the vision of evangelism and starting churches, and he asked if he could stay another year as he had caught the vision of what we were doing. So now his second year was nearly finished, so he finished and returned to America. But he went straight to flying school as he was hoping to become a missionary pilot for us and our new outreach. We had found two people groups that were completely unreached, and we were hoping to reach them within the next two years by aircraft. In flying school, he did his work very well. As when he was working with us, he also did an excellent piece of work in whatever he did. So I think about mid-1996, he left Nsonga and went back to America, and I remained alone at the mission and continued to build the new mission.

Growing Up

N ow to get back to my book. I know I'm very far on behind. I have to work hard to get along with the story; otherwise, it will take a long time.

When I was a child growing up, things were very different then. I remember Mother taking us to the store to buy some food and some things in the store as small children. It was during World War II, and things were not easy to buy. Most things were known not to be available at that time. It was hard to buy just a simple thing like sugar. You had to have special tokens which would buy sugar. Often, the commodity was not available. There are many things during that period of time that were very, very difficult to obtain. I remember how we used to keep those as very special because we all loved sugar. We tried to be very careful not to lose any sugar pennies as we called them so we could buy sugar when we went to the store. Most of what was available at that time was called corn sugar, and that is all we had to use. It was not the proper sugar, but it was a good substitute. I think at that point of time, there were only the three of us boys who were alive. I do not think that my brother Sam was born yet at that time. During that time, Uncle Uri had chickens in the chicken house, my mother had chickens in the other end of the barn, and Dad was caring for the cows in the cow stable in the barn. I do not recall any other animals except horses and mules, which we used for driving and farming. I do not remember that Dad had other animals except some sheep that Grandfather Stoltzfus had. He had a large herd of sheep that every day were taken to the graveyard or the cemetery, where they would graze on the grass to keep the cemetery looking mowed. Sheep are good grass mowers, and they keep the grass down. Taking these sheep out to the cemetery each day was something that I love to be a part of as we walked the sheep up on the road about two hundred feet to the cemetery fence and then put them in to graze. One thing I remember very well is that there was a male, Ram, as we used to call him, the sheep buck. He used to like to attack me since I was just a small boy. I remember many times when he would come after me, I would lay in the ditch on my back and kick at him. I was deathly afraid of him. Hey, he was not a friend of mine, I hated the old sheep buck.

Even though life was hard and things were difficult to get during the war, we were young and didn't know or understand the hard experiences of life during war. So we would go on. Dad and Mother had a horse and buggy. That is how we traveled when we went to town or went anywhere. When Granddad would go to a nearby town, he would get a neighbor to take him with his car and then pay him for the journey. I was always preparing for these trips to town. Nothing was done foolishly as things were very expensive and hard to come by. I remember one time when we were coming home from church driving in the horse and carriage, a big truck came by and spooked the horse. Suddenly, we went dashing off the road. The horse ran through a cornfield and then back onto the road again. It was quite some excitement for us little kids to see how a horse conducted himself when he himself is scared.

Being very young, of course, we never knew what danger was, so we would do many foolish things like children do as we were growing up. Every morning and evening, Dad would be milking the cows and reading the Word of God. He was ordained into the church or ministry just a few years before, and he now had to learn what the Word of God said and how he was to preach the Word of God! That was a big and heavy responsibility on Dad's shoulders. And Dad did a good job of trying to learn. As we were growing up, again and again, we would hear Dad when he was milking the cows by hand. He was quoting scripture verse by verse memorizing it by the chapter. This was the work of my father as we were growing up. I remember he was able to "quote whole Bible chapters," as he had learned them by heart. Those were the days, not like today, but that is in the past. Dad passed away in 1995.

As for me as I was growing up, life is always a challenge, and we always wanted to do everything that we could do to make life easier. That was a challenge. For the people around us, life was not easy, it was not ideal. Therefore, we would work hard at what we did to prove ourselves an advantage. Most of what I remember was that life is challenging, but we had a lot of fun. I remember one time when my brother was naughty and Uncle Uri got so annoyed with him that he put him inside an empty feed bag and tied the bag shut. He then put him in the upstairs barn den and left him hang there for some time. He then took him down again and left him out. Of course, he went running to Mother and complained how Uncle had been so bad to him.

Such were the pranks and the thing that us boys just had to get into and the things that we had to suffer because of our own stupidity, as intelligent young boys are and do. I do not remember much about working in the fields in those days because we were just young boys, but yes, we were growing up and more ambitious every day, and then we were only ambitious, but we became rambunctious, and that was at a great price because we had to be disciplined as we were learning how to live in a society of more people than just us. Does that sound like boys?

It wasn't a long time before we learned that we were a challenge to the community. Granddad Stoltzfus was a man of integrity, and he lived at the home farm. Where my father was staying was on the second farm that Granddad bought during the time of the Depression. At that time, most people were losing their farm by bankruptcy because of the depression. Things were difficult, and it was hard times, but Granddad was able to buy the second farm. He lost his own barn by lightning striking the barn, and he lost his own food, hay, etc. I think it was 1936, because of his relationship with God and his commitment to serve God with his whole heart, even though it was hard times, Granddad excelled and went forward.

I remember Granddad had the only steam engine in the Conestoga Valley. He had his own sawmill that he turned with the steam engine. Things went well with Granddad in everything that he did.

I remember when the war was over, Granddad would go to sales and buy up all the sewing machines that he could buy. He would bring them home, put them in his workshop, and go over them and repair them. Then he would give them to needy families that needed a sewing machine to make their own clothing. Granddad was a very generous individual and a very hard worker. He taught his children to work very hard as well, and that is where we developed our work ethics. This was the example that Granddad lived by. He was nobody's joke. He was an example of integrity. That is what he taught everyone that knew him: integrity. Integrity number 1, integrity number 2, number 3 also was integrity! He was such an example that many people wanted to follow his way of life.

I remembered many, many times riding with him, and Roy his horse and spring wagon. We would go to visit the neighbors or just doing work on the farm. I think I had an advantage, more than my siblings, because my name was Stephen. That was the name of Granddad also. Therefore, I was with him many, many, many times in my younger years until I was five years old.

Time went on, and I was growing up. Many times, I just loved and cherished the times I could have with Granddad. I think I have many stories that my other siblings and many other people never had the opportunity to learn from Granddad like I did. I remember when Granddad would go up into the barn and get hay down for the cows. Hay was passing down the hay hole. It was constant until it was enough. Then he would get silage for the cows to eat. He would work so fast that silage was coming down the silo shoot constantly until it was enough to feed the cows. He was known to do things quickly.

I remember he used to have many beehives, many hives with honey. This was my greatest delight. Granddad realized that I like honey like no one else. He soon had to make rules for me to be able to enjoy my honey. I was very messy with honey on my bread. It would run off and make a sticky mess everywhere. So Granddad said, "If you want honey on your bread, it may not run off. Otherwise, you don't have honey on your bread."

I very quickly conquered that stipulation. I would take a knife, put a big wad of honey on my bread, then put that piece of bread in my mouth, and bite it off before the honey runs off. Granddad would look at me, and he said, "Boy, do you like honey?" I would get another wad of honey on my knife, put it on the next bite on the bread, and bite it off before it ran off the bread. Yes, I conquered that stipulation.

Someone that really enjoys what he is doing, Granddad said I was such a challenge to him. He had to look after me sitting in the Amish church. Dad was now a minister in the church, so Granddad would have to look after me since my father was busy with his new ministry. To look after me was not a cup of tea, as I was a chore, not only a chore, but I was a handful of chores. Granddad said when we were in church, "Hold yourself still." I could not do that. That was not me. Granddad said, "When I would make sure that you would not be able to go under the bench in the front, you would slip down under the bench from the back. You were not difficult, you were a handful of difficulties." I was a challenge to Granddad, and to everyone else that was sitting around Granddad, I was a fidgety live wire to put it in mild terms. This is how we were growing up, and I was the nutcase that had to be dealt with.

During charismatic renewal in the seventies, we would hear the term some people are a nut case, and I would say, "When you crack that nut, it contains a lot of good meat." Therefore, I was always a challenge to my parents. Do you know what I think, I grew up somehow, at least a little bit. Maybe the rest is still in question. We will have to see by the end of the book if the question is still there, ha ha!

I do remember my mother telling me that one day, I fell down the hay hole and broke my collarbone. I do not remember this, but I was told I was always getting into trouble in one way or another. Is it a wonder than that this young innovative person always getting in trouble would one day become a missionary in the land of a foreign country? Far in the bush and far away from the city.

When we returned to America, we felt for this time it was mission accomplished. So during this period of time in America, I decided to do one year of Bible school. So I registered at Elim Bible

Institute, and we moved to Lima, New York, and started Bible school in 1980. When we finished one year there, we again moved back to Pennsylvania and prepared to go to the country of Zaire as I was getting letters from a church there that was asking us to come and work with them. Brother Luke Weaver was having a missionary convention at his church, and he asked us to come and be with him at this meeting at Grace Chapel. So we went, I think it was about April or June that year. Ruth at this point said, "I need to hear from God, or I am not going to Africa." The speaker was from Bradenton, Florida. He did not know the Fishers. He was speaking at the meeting when suddenly he turned to the right side of the building and came walking back the aisle. He walked right up to sister Ruth and began to prophesy over her. She went out like a light, she fell onto the floor. And there God spoke to her. When she got up forty-five minutes later, she said, "Sweetheart, we need to go to Africa." I already knew that. But this was her answer. So we finished our process, and again, we prepared to depart and go to the unknown! What a mighty God we serve. Mighty, he is, and forever shall be. Hallelujah! God is God always and forever! Amen!

But Zaire is not easy, as it is a very large country. It has the same square miles, as the United States east of the Mississippi River, one country that size with a spoiled economy. At that time, the president was the wealthiest monarch in the world. But his country did not have thieves; theft was not heard of. As a military government, he said all bandits die. And so it was. When we went to Zaire, the value of their money was seven and a half Zaire's to the U.S. dollar. Then the entire bottom fell out of the monetary system. And twelve years later, it was eighty-four million Zaire's to one dollar, completely unbelievable but very real. But in spite of difficulties and problems, the work of God flourished. God is God. Hallelujah!

Remember for the first six months, we did not drive there with our vehicle. We left the vehicle at a Catholic mission in Kasenga. We then traveled thirteen hours by riverboat to our new home right on a beautiful big river full of crocodiles and hippopotamus. One evening, we went out on the river with a spotlight and a battery. We must have seen one thousand crocodiles. All along the banks, they were lined up. We could see the lineup of eyes like LED lights. There were many. We knew the river was full of crocodiles.

Our dear daughter Anita thought she had to be like all the other African children that stand in the water knee-deep to fish by pole. She loved to do that very much. She would catch her own fish. She would clean them herself, then fry them herself, and then eat them herself. She was a special girl. But I wanted my special girl longer than just today. So I told her no more fishing standing in the water. Again and again, I found her doing the same thing until one time I reminded her for the last time. I took the stick of correction and warmed her backside firmly. Then she understood what I was trying to say. I did not want her taken by a crocodile. But she was a child, only five years old. And she liked to do what other five-year-olds do. She learned from the children, that was good, but I wanted her to live one day more. So she stopped that.

October 29, news brief

I feel compelled this evening to report to you the burden that God has put on my heart. We are living in a time of crisis. We need to know our covenant relationship with God the Father, and we need to be aware of the times and the seasons in which we are presently living.

In the book of Daniel chapter 11 and verse 36 to 37, it says this: "As for the king, he shall have all his own ways, in his pride he will think himself a match for any god, even of that God, he boasts himself the rival. Who is above all other gods! And still he shall thrive, vengeance is not yet ready to overtake him. Doom shall come when doom is due. What are his father's Gods to him? Woman's dalliance is all that concerns him; of gods, he regards little, that he will set himself up over all of them." Wow! What a picture. We are living in times of peril, but they are exciting times. For the saints of God, it is near the time of redemption!

For me here at Rolling Fields, I am soon coming to my last day here, as Sunday morning the sixth of November, I will be leaving this place and returning to the Lancaster area and staying with my son. Scott Merritt, myself, Randy, Anita, and Daniel Chisabwe will leave and go to Africa to carry out the wishes of my precious wife and allow her burial resting place to be at the mission where she served and lived since 2000.

It will not be easy for me to return with her being absent as she was always by my side. So thank you for your prayers. We will make it!

Memorial services are planned, and we will carry them out when we get there. The day after we arrive, we will have a memorial service in the capital city. Your prayers are very much coveted. Many people in the capital knew her. Then we want to visit the mission where we served from 1969 until 1972 then visit the most famous place that she loved so much, Victoria Falls.

That is the place where a thief, some years ago, grabbed her handbag and ran off, carrying with it her precious dentures. Only a thief could be so successful. He got no money, only her teeth and those he could not use. Ha ha!

Then we will go to the Copper Belt Providence to the Chibangu Mission where she had served since the year 2000 and there have a memorial service. All this to say, it is an emotionally hard time for me. Thank you for your prayers.

I think I am doing very well. Again, thank you for your prayers.

I will be speaking at the Full Gospel Businessmen's meeting on Saturday the evening of the fifth. So this week, I will have to pack up and prepare to leave Sunday morning. That will be the end of my stay here for the present time.

Everyone here is asking when I am coming back as my family here is going to be missing me. This has become my home for the present time. And people have a hard time accepting that I will be leaving for the next three months. Where God will lead me to next is yet to be seen. My life is not my own.

I only know that God is not finished with me yet and that he has commissioned me to rise up a home for unwed mothers in Africa. Thank you for praying for me. I will share the detail as it comes to be known. I only know for sure, God is not finished with me yet.

I will stay in touch, hopefully on a weekly basis. Thank you and God bless you abundantly, Stephen.

October 30

To refresh my memory as I am writing this book, I have reread the old newsletter from 2001. That was the year we had fifty-six students in school already. I needed to build a new school.

During the previous year and up until October, we built a new building for the orphans. It was built to house about fifteen orphans. Orphans are everywhere, and all needed help. They were beginning to come, and we were still building it with compressed bricks which were made on site.

Trying to teach our workers to lay bricks using a level to keep their wall upright was a hard task. I do not understand why this is such a hard task, but they insist on laying bricks without using a level. I went to look at one of the end walls that they had put up. At the far end of the building, the wall is nearly as high as the peak; they have not used the level.

The top of the wall was now six inches off level. The wall is near to fall down. So I quickly grabbed the chain saw. I cut an eight-inch tree, about sixteen feet long, and propped it against the wall that was now going to fall down to keep the end of the building from falling down.

That night, it rained. For the lack of cement, we laid our bricks, eight-inch block size, with dirt from the anthill and not cement. Now the whole wall was in danger. The mud had not yet set nor dried. Now the whole building was in danger. But God is amazing, so very amazing.

The next morning, the wall was still standing. Everything was in order, and it was not going to fall down. We finished the building. It took a few weeks to build. Now finally, it was time to put the roof on. So we got the roof on. The building was safe and was not going to fall down.

The windows were taken from an old farmhouse in America where they had put in plastic frame windows in place of the wooden frames. We put in the container the wood frame windows, and then we used them in the orphanage. This is how we saved money. Now the building was safe. And our carpenter was busy putting bunk beds in each room.

The orphans can now move into the new orphanage. The work was hard, and the days were long. But our workmen were loyal. And they too worked very hard. So now we have a beautiful building for the orphan.

Again, we were busy with the sawmill, cutting wood for the doors and wood for the beds. The grind was still on, and we continued to make what we needed. At the same time, there was a lot of work to be done; the toilets had to be built. The guesthouse was in progress. There was lots of building to be done.

More trees had to be taken out so that we had room for the buildings. We soon learned that more trees had to be taken out so that when storms come and trees blow down that they will not fall on to a building.

It was making room for fresh hope for our children. They had no one that could help them. They were a happy bunch of children. Every day, all the children came to prayers as we started the day to ask our God for guidance for the day. We realize we were not alone and that we needed his help.

At that time, we were so very busy with the skid loader. We used it to dig the dirt to make the bricks, which we then used to build, also used the skid loader with the backhoe on the front to dig our pits for the latrines. The skid loader was a needed piece of equipment for building.

Everything we had was used to the max as we were very busy building. We were building three buildings at the same time. We were building the orphanage and the toilets for the orphanage. The guesthouse was also under construction, and we were building the clinic. So the first year we were there, there was a lot of construction going on. At the same time, we were also finishing the house, which was our residence. There was a lot happening at the same time. If I remember correctly, we had about eighteen men working for us in the building. At the same time, we were also clearing land for fields, so we would be able to grow our own food. However at this time, we did not have a tractor. That only arrived in 2005. So there was a lot of construction going on, and the place was growing very quickly. The first two years, we did the tilling of the soil for three acres with an industrial diesel rototiller. Anyway, we used that until we wore it out. God was so good to give us the things that we needed. Again, what can we say, God is so amazing and so awesome. Hallelujah! What a mighty God we serve. If you do not believe in God, that's okay. He is there anyway! My Bible says, "The fool has said in his heart there is no God, he made heaven and earth and all that is within it. Believe it or not, He is there!"

Building a New Mission

As soon as bricks were made, we wanted to start to put up new buildings. Now we were living up in the mountains. And at night, it was very cold. And in the early morning coming to work to make bricks was no man's desire, as the mud that had to be mixed and was done by walking around in the mud. And it was ice cold. And there were only two boys that they would do that early in the morning. The others were not interested because it was so cold. But Ngala and Chicholacoso were the only two men that would tramp the mud first thing in the morning because they got cold feet. But these two men did a good job, and they used to do this first thing in the morning to make some mud for the bricks. Then we would put this mud into brick molds as measured eight inches wide, and six inches deep, and ten inches long. The bricks were very heavy. But in those days, they only built our muscles. And the building went up very fast as with this brick, it covered a lot of territory. So we began to do our building after we've made bricks. But first to make bricks, lay them out on the ground to dry then stack them into a kiln and bake them with fire and then burn a whole trees in the kiln. Yes, it is a lot of hard work, but then we had a good brick to build the mission. At my age, I would find an easier way not because it would not be a good way, but I cannot work like that now, and now we have a brick machine. So the fact being is that we only had a short dry season, three months in total. And we had to have all the bricks made and burned. Boy, did we work! And the blessing of God was with us; somehow, we always have food, and the work flourished.

During the time when we were making bricks, we also had built a temporary clinic. Mom was busy every day in the clinic. This was Mom's place. And it was her chosen profession. And it's where she exceled. All kinds of illnesses came to the clinic: lacerations, burned bodies, and—most of all—malaria. Malaria was the biggest killer of them all. But Mother never complained as she ministered to these needs. She puts up with a lot of inconveniences as she did not have things convenient. And she worked very hard eight hours a day in the clinic. Frequently, we would come with cut fingers. With a grateful heart, she would continue to work and minister to people with all kind of the illnesses. Then this little girl was brought in by a wheelbarrow ambulance, she had a broken femur in her right leg. You did not have many broken bones, but there were some. So while Mom was looking after the afflicted and the sick and the needy people, we were beginning to lay the foundations of the buildings now in a new place and a new area in the mountains. It was gorgeously beautiful.

So about five times a year, we would go to South Africa to get supplies. I had to stop in Zimbabwe as we have friends that had a business of repairing microscopes. The gentleman that fixed the microscopes said he knows a man in town who sells dumpy levels, so I went to him and ask him how much I have to pay for a dumpy level. I think if I remember correctly, I paid $125 for it. It was a surveyor's level that was used on the mines. It was a very good and precision machine. One time, it had cost a lot of money. So I bought it and used it for building my buildings. With it, I made straight roads. And I leveled up my buildings. It was a beautiful piece of technology. It was such an instrument of blessing. With this instrument, I would also make right angles. It was such a special machine. And so we began to put in the foundations of the building. And walls on the buildings began to rise. Progress was on the way, summertime had come out again. And now making bricks was not so cold. We worked very hard as we constructed the building. We had to haul all our bricks with the Unimog. We worked long hard days.

Oh, let man declare this day, stand up and be counted, for Jesus Christ is Lord of lord, and forever will be King of kings! Hallelujah!"

So being joyfully overwhelmed, we left that small city. Chef Kalala was with us. He said, "You see, these people did not consider God, and so they have failed. So now what you do, you go back home, pick up the pieces, and keep on moving forward and finish the project that you have started."

When we arrived back at the mission, these dear friends have already started to do their own thing. They told all the villagers in the whole area that we were never coming back and that they are here to stay and they are going to take over the work. Now we returned, and we took over as usual, much of the work we had to do by ourselves, as no one wanted to help us. They had given many gifts to the people who had nothing, who were not able to buy salt and sugar except that from the mission store. They literally gave fifty pounds of sugar and fifty pounds of salt, clothing and shoes, and pots and pans and whatever they could to bribe the people and to win their favor. They did a good job of it. So after about one week going by, no one wanted to help us to build the new mission except one boy had come. He was the son of a prostitute. And he was not easily swayed by the smooth talk of these people. His name was Kalenga. And he came and helped us. And we talked to him about that we need more help. So that evening when he went home from work, he did something on his own. He went to talk to the chief. The chief by this time had made a commitment to Jesus Christ. And he was very happy with the work that we were doing. So the chief called a community meeting. And he explained to the people how that these traitors that came to work with us were telling them lies about us and that he had given this land to us and not to these other people and said they were not going to take over. He set everyone straight on the situation. I never could have accomplished this without the chief's help, and I think at this time, this great problem was behind us. And from that time on, we went forward. He told the chief no one wants to come to work for us. So the chief came the next day and talked to the people and said these people had left and taking their possessions. And they went away and left us in perfect peace, and we experienced the tremendous blessing of God, and we returned to build a new mission that we had started, and we didn't even finished the house at that time. As when these folks left, they left their dirty trace follow only for a short time. As they were soon forgotten, the chief was a staunch supporter. So when the local people refused to show up to work, the chief talked to them and told them those people were traitors and they were not good people and that they should support the work that we are doing. It may be that it took one month until the lies had turned sour. And the reality of the truth was revealed. And we were up and running again. It was just a long sad story. But praise the Lord, we have learned through it, and we shall prosper forever because of it. Jesus said, "If you do not forgive those who trespass against you, neither will your heavenly father forgive you" (Matt. 6:15). The church also was much stronger. And God did many great miracles in our midst all the time. I don't remember which building we built next. First, the small house then the big house then we had left the big house for a time as these people had left. I think next we build the hospital. That was a big necessary accomplishment. The first building we worked on was the workshop and the big storeroom with the office on top of the workshop on the second floor. The work was going forward, and the rain had come. I remember we had to work very hard to get buildings finished before the rain sets in. And we could not get cement at the time, so we were using anthill dirt which is also a very solid material to work with in place of cement. It worked well, it just did not dry as fast. And we had to hurry as we were putting on a grass roof as tin roofing. It was very expensive, so we completed the workshop and office with grass roof. Then we placed tin roof over the outside of the workshop. The whole storeroom also had tin roof which we did not have the money for tin over the office area so that is why we did the office in grass. Grass is also more delightful, it is cooler in the summertime, and it is warmer in the wintertime. And this grass roof was there thirteen years and still was in very good shape. So there is nothing wrong with a grass roof, just you cannot have it under a tree where a tree will be weeping water on it as a constant drip of water on the roof will root the grass. So that covered my office space and then workshop.

On the side of the workshop was a tin roof, which acted as a porch next to the workshop as an extra workshop space, the whole storage area. And then this was our storeroom. The whole storeroom I had built with broken bricks that were not used for building the house. The storeroom walls were about seven feet high with a flat roof on top. And it served its purpose well. I remember we used to have such a terrible problem in the storeroom with rats. It was a dirt floor, and the rats dug holes everywhere. And many times, we found a snake in the storeroom, as they were busy catching rats, and I was okay with that as not all snakes are enemies. But sometimes, it was a spitting cobra. And that is not okay, and they also have a venomous bite. Rat poison we could not get, so I made my own. I took the gas sulfur tablets that we used to kill insects in corn and beans and whatever these weevils would get into. This one particular gas tablet, we would use to treat corn. So I said if it kills weevils, maybe it will kill rats. So I remember going to experiment with the anything for everything. So I took three gas tablets, crushed them to powder, and put it into cornflower that we used to use to make porridge. Wow, to my amazement, I mixed it into the meal, and the next morning, there were no rats at all. There were no rats running anywhere, only a sound of rats croaking. They were coughing, they were growling, but no rats anywhere. They were all gone. Unbelievable. It really worked. And so we graciously got rid of the rat population. I know we know how to get rid of rats now.

So after, we had the workshop built and the bedroom for Mom, and I was in the office area as we did not yet have our house built, so we moved from our tent to the office as the storeroom was finished. Then Mahlon's bedroom was upstairs where Mom and I were sleeping in the room which was known as my office but it was also a bedroom. And if guests came, they would sleep there also. It was a bit crammed, but it would offer a good night sleep. And that office was where all our technical electric electronic work was done. I had a small gas soldering irons there. And all our electrical fittings were done in this office. I had put a stairway going up to the office. It was a different kind of building for the bush, as two-story buildings are not found there. Next, we started to build the hospital. That structure and building was much greater. It was about this time the medical work had grown into a huge work. Mom was an excellent doctor.

She had a lot of experience. She was such a beautiful person. Patients would come from all the way across the mountain. Some said they walked three days to get there. They would always bring a gift for the medicine. Most of all, our medical work was done on the barter system. They would bring a bag of beans, or a half a bag of corn, or a chicken or a goat in payment for the medicine, for they have no money to pay for medicine. Money was inflating so fast in Zaire. No one could put a price on things with money. So it was much more reliable through payment with animals, or chicken, or with food to eat. So the work continued to grow, and we completed the hospital.

In one year during this time of hospital work, Mama was doing a lot of deliveries. Many people came to the hospital to give birth to a child. Mom was known very well as someone to deliver the baby. The other big things that you had on the daily basis was malaria, more malaria cases. We were still very busy developing the mission. However in 1990, I got the sawmill. I have been looking at a sawmill because that is what we need to do our building. Many people showed me portable sawmills. And I began to look around when we arrived in America. There were many different brand names we looked at. Then one time when I was at Indianapolis, someone took me to Woodmizer Sawmill Factory. I talked to the president of the company. As he sat down and had lunch with me, his parents came here as Polish refugees. And what a beautiful brother he was. We talked for some time. Then he said we would qualify to get one as a gift. But he said their gifts were given through an organization from California. So I flew to California to talk to this organization's office. But they refused to recognize me as a viable mission. I do not know what their problem was. But they would not donate me a mill. It is a long story. But they would not give me a mill. So I returned to the office and Indianapolis. And again, I talked with the president. He was grossly annoyed. And he said this, "I have had enough of complaints about this organization. Therefore, we will not again give that organization another mill, as we have complaints about their administration. But for you, Mr. Fisher, you qualified to have a free mill donated to you, and since they refuse to give you a sawmill to use for your mission work, they will get no more donations from us.

But since you qualify, I will personally donate a saw mill to you and your organization."

So he donated one to us, Project Redemption Ministries, an LT 40 sawmill, and we made plans to have it transported via container to Zaire. It was hard times in Zaire. But God made a way for us to do a great work, and when the container reached Zaire, they unloaded everything and put it in the state warehouse. And that was where we picked up the goods from. But then they stole my container, loaded with copper, and sent it to South Africa to the port. But I lost the container. Such is life in the bush. But they decided to retrieve my shipment, including the sawmill, praise the lord! And the sawmill was such a tremendous instrument of blessing as we cut timber and made a number of big things for the hospital and the home.

Zaire had about ten different kinds of hardwood and gorgeously beautiful, blood red wood with black grain. It was nice it was beautiful, and we made many beautiful things out of wood. I made one huge picnic table out of a tree that was lying on the ground and was dried and well seasoned. It was 4.8 m long that was nearly a 14-foot table, again gorgeously beautiful and extremely heavy. So much so that six people could not carry it. And then we built a new mission up on top of a huge hill. It was a very beautiful area up in the mountains. When we looked to so west of this location, we would see a beautiful waterfall. That was just a beautiful location. There we started to build a new mission. I cut posts twenty-one feet long and planted them four feet into the ground. If I remember correctly, I have planned eighteen of these posts thirty-six feet of this long building on the first floor, what is for the living quarters. Underneath was for storage. On the end of the building was for storing the vehicles and workshop. If we could have finished it and it would have been one beautiful structure, all the material was cut out by this sawmill. It was a fourteen-horse gas engine. But still it is a beautiful job. I talked to the manufacture of the sawmill and asked why they don't have a diesel engine on the sawmill. I kept pestering them about a diesel motor for the sawmill as gas was so expensive and hard to get. Finally, they begin to build them with diesel motors on them. And what an improvement this was. When the war came and swept us out of the country, we already had our new mission building, about half completed roof is on half of the building, and the main structure was half constructed. So we were making good progress. I remember when I went to buy the iron sheets and we went to pay for $1,500 worth of roofing material. I went to the bank to get the money. At that time, they had printed money notes worth five million in one note, as the money had devaluated so much. My friend reversed his Mercedes-Benz up to the door of the bank. And we had four suitcases full of money, and many more boxes filled with bills, and it filled up his trunk and the back seat of the car, and we drove to the merchant. And we began to count the money. It was so many bills that it took us two hours and forty-five minutes to count the money. Only later that evening, when we were finished counting the money, did we then load up the roofing sheets and drive to the guesthouse parking lot, which was walled in an area that was supposed to be safe. Such were the early days of Zaire. This was 1996. Now I am told things are very different today. I would love to go back and see the place today. But I was held hostage there for ten days, and the church has asked me to not return as they fear for my life.

As a young man that was growing up in the village of Kashiobwe, when we arrived there in 1982, he was fifteen years old and grew up in that village. He has today become governor of the city of Lubumbashi and governor of the entire province of Katanga and will probably be the next president of the country. The existing government has caused him to go into exile for his own safety. When we reached the village of Kashiobwe, he was fifteen years old, and our son was eighteen years old, and the two were good friends together at that time. His name was Moses Katumbe. His father was a Jew from Italy. And his mother was a local Bemba woman from that village. Moses seemed to be one of the most intelligent children of the family. I also knew other brothers and sisters of Moses. And they were just like other normal villagers. But Moses was very clever and intelligent, and he grew up to be a sharp businessman. And he did very well in business and became very wealthy. He was a hardworking young man and grew up in the Catholic faith. And he had many friends and was a friend of ours during those days. He even wanted to marry my daughter. So she was much younger than him. He was a friend of the family.

Now we took the roof sheets to Nsonga and began to put a the new building. This was the roof sheets that we paid so many bills for, a whole Mercedes-Benz trunk full plus boxes in the back seat, this expensive roofing for our building, that took two and a half hours to count all the money. That is how useless the currency has become. They gave as much as five million notes as possible, and the rest was given in smaller notes, and that's why it took forever to count it. I hope America will never have to get to be in a situation like this, but we have lived it in Zaire, again in Zambia, and now today also in Zimbabwe.

So count your blessings, my dear friends, because I see the handwriting on the wall. We have been there, and we have done that. I do not ask anyone to experience what we have experienced. So now we were in the process of building a new mission on top of the mountain range. I have great dreams for their area. Inside Zaire, there were lakes and rivers everywhere. As I looked down from the high mountain ranges, there was a river flowing through the valley. At the far end of the valley, there were two mountain ranges coming right out to where the river flowed through. I looked at the valley over to the left, there was a waterfall coming down from the mountain range. Another river flowing over into the valley and where the river left this area, it was an ideal place to build a dam. And being a dreamer, I said I would like to dam the river with those two mountain ranges coming together. It was only about two hundred feet wide.   And it would have backed up a huge dam, an excellent ideal place for hydroelectric. Yes, I am a dreamer if I can make life better for people in a situation. That is my passion. So on top of this high mountain range, we were now constructing a new mission. We did not know that it was going to be short-lived. We worked very hard, and construction was very beautiful. But in 1996, it all came to an abrupt end, as another war broke out in the country and a rebel leader that was a Muslim came and fought again the existing military government and brought this government to an end. And he took over the country. It is a long story, but I will try to recapture it and tell you the story the best that I can.

To recapture a story is not always easy. During our time of ministry in Zaire, we also experienced a multitude of miracles again and again and again. Miracles were the order of the day, let me just relate to a few of them. In the hospital, Ruth always experienced miracles probably more in the hospital than out on the field. Although in training pastors and establishing churches, there were many, many miracles also. All these experiences were a time of blessing. Pastors would come to pastors meeting four or five days every month and to teaching sessions, and they had no shoes to wear. These were the average people of the bush. They did not own shoes, they had a good heart, and that was of a much greater value than shoes. If they had any kind of shoes, they were made out of tire. But they would walk for miles. Two come to the meeting point where we were having a seminar. And the response was always positive. They were determined to have the blessing of God. My good wife, who has delivered hundreds of babies and has now gone to be with Jesus, has been the instrument and witness of the great and mighty work of the Holy Ghost. She has been the instrument to bring healing to extreme and violent burns. She has sutured many violent and in extreme lacerations.

I remember one time a man came in, saying, "Come quickly and get my uncle before he dies." Usually, we did not go on an ambulance calls as we did not have the extra fuel. But this time, we went to get this man. He was plowing with two oxen and a walking plow. I guess there was a lot of grass and weeds he was trying to plow under. Then he stepped on top of the weeds to get them to turn over by the plow and then become covered." When he tripped, his foot went down, and he pushed the weeds under the plow, and the point of the plow caught in the front of his foot, at the ankle, the plow cut the front of his ankle wide open. What a gory mess. We put him into the SUV and quickly transported him to the hospital. He had just lost so much blood he was nearly unconscious. Mom then elevated his feet higher than his head to get the blood flowing into his brain. So he would not collapse into unconsciousness. And then she began to suture the terrible wound. To our examination, we did not find any bones broken, so we sutured him up. And after three weeks, he went home.

This is just one of the many. Mom was always calm and collected in a situation like this. She was one excellent doctor. She always did an excellent job.

Ruth's Testimony of Child Raised from the Dead

One day, I was working at the workshop, I think that I was sharpening saw blades for the sawmill. And a patient came running from the hospital. "Dad, Mommy is calling you. She needs your help quickly."

And Mommy said this, "I am tired of delivering dead babies. There have been too many young girls pregnant. And their pelvic passage is just too small to deliver babies. At the age of thirteen, fourteen, and fifteen, I have just delivered the baby for Petto, the daughter of our beloved prayer warrior. She is fifteen years old and has experienced a two-day delivery. One hour ago, the baby had a healthy heart peace but with a very hard delivery. The baby delivered dead. But there have been just too many like this. We are going to pray. We are asking God to make this dead baby alive. It shall live. I'm tired of delivering dead babies. Let us pray!"

All the staff were called. And the pastor was called. And we were in deep prayer and talking to the Creator about restoring life to this dead baby. Everyone was in deep sorrow as we knew this family very well. And this child was as though it was the child of our own. Ruth said, "Enough is enough." And we prayed, and we prayed, and we prayed some more for at least forty-five minutes or an hour. We were in prayer, and asking the Lord to put life into this child again. Finally in desperation, Mom picked up that dead child from the table and held the child above her head, shaking as she spoke, and she said this, now shouting loudly, "Devil, you will not have this child. This child shall live and be normal. I am tired of delivering dead babies. This child shall live, this child shall live, in the name of Jesus, life come into this child. In the name of Jesus, give back the life to this child. Just a few hours ago, it had a healthy heartbeat, give me back my child!"

She brought the child down and laid it on the table. She turned to the mother, and she was ready to say, and the child began to cry. What she was ready to say was, "My dear sister, I have done all I can do, but your child is dead" But in that instance, the child began to cry. There was joy, there was rejoicing, as the child was returned to the mother and then passed for the grandmother to hold. Everyone was overjoyed as they had never seen anything like this. There was great joy in the camp. And soon, people came from everywhere to celebrate! Great is the Lord, and greatly to be praised. Hallelujah! Hallelujah! Amen.

This same experience was witnessed on three occasions. Yes, three children came back to life after having been born dead. We served an awesome God! And he is greatly to be praised. Amen and amen!

Mom was giving her testimony of God's amazing grace in Africa. She testified how a baby girl was born dead, as many children were, as many of the girls were too young to give birth, as they were from age thirteen through fifteen years, as she related the story, when she was telling the people how this baby had been born dead and after forty-five minutes of prayer, and travail, it came to life again. In this huge audience, this great big sea of people, there was a well-learned doctor. In the audience, after Mom was finished giving her testimony, this doctor stood up, and he said and in a loud voice as he did not have a microphone, "Madam, if that baby was dead for forty-five minutes, then for sure, it had brain damage. For anyone being dead that length of time and then come to life has brain damage."

And then perhaps it was the boldest statement my wife ever made. They said, she quickly turned halfway around looking directly at the doctor and addressed him, "Sir, have you ever seen God do a half job? This child today is five years old. And it is normal and going to school. And since then, this miracle has taken place two times more. Two more children were born dead and have come back to life as we have prayed. God is an awesome God!"

About the Author

B orn into an Amish family on July 18, 1941, third born out of ten children, I grew up full of energy and creating quite a challenge for my siblings and my parents, and then at age eight—lapsed into sickness, called rheumatic fever—I was bedfast for one year. I heard the doctor say to my dad, "This boy will never work a day in his life." I was ill for four years and had to repeat grade four in school as my illness caused me to lose one year of school. Then at age twelve, the Lord healed me. And I again began to live a normal life. Turning sixteen, I began to follow a Christian youth group. There I came to faith in Jesus Christ. And I began to desire to win souls for Jesus. At age eighteen, I said to Dad, "We have to evangelize our youth, as they are lost."

Dad said, "The Amish do not do that."

I said, "Then I am in the wrong church." I left the Amish at age nineteen and then became a missionary. In February 1963. We left for Africa and served Zambia, Zaire, and Zimbabwe. We were there until December 2015. My wife worked in the medical field by my side then graduated with honors in July 2016. And at present, I am residing at Welsh Mountain Home.

Stephen S Fisher

CPSIA information can be obtained
at www.ICGtesting.com
Printed in the USA
BVHW081914140220
572128BV00001B/64